T0316848

Crisis and Sustainability

SOFIA CONFERENCES
ON SOCIAL
AND ECONOMIC
DEVELOPMENT
IN EUROPE

Edited by
Prof. Dr. George Chobanov
Prof. Dr. Jürgen Plöhn
Prof. Dr. Horst Schellhaass

Volume 4

George Chobanov
Jürgen Plöhn
(eds.)

Crisis and Sustainability: Responses from Different Positions

14th Annual Conference of the Faculty
of Economics and Business Administration

Sofia, 7-8 October 2011

Bibliographic Information published by the Deutsche Nationalbibliothek
The Deutsche Nationalbibliothek lists this publication in the Deutsche
Nationalbibliografie; detailed bibliographic data is available in the internet at
http://dnb.d-nb.de.

Cover illustrations:
Printed with kind permission
of the universities of Cologne and Sofia.

Library of Congress Cataloging-in-Publication Data

Crisis and sustainability : responses from different positions, 14th Annual
Conference of the Faculty of Economics and Business Administration Sofia, 7-8
October 2011 / George Chobanov, Jürgen Plöhn (eds.).
pages cm
ISBN 978-3-631-64062-3 (print) — ISBN 978-3-653-03807-1 (e-book)
1. Financial crises—Europe—Congresses. 2. Sustainable development—
Europe—Congresses. 3. Europe—Economic policy—Congresses.
4. Europe—Social policy—Congresses.
I. Chobanov, George, 1948- editor. II. Plöhn, Jürgen, editor.
HB3782.C755 2013
338.94—dc23

2013037144

ISSN 1867-562X
ISBN 978-3-631-64062-3 (Print)
E-ISBN 978-3-653-03807-1 (E-Book)
DOI 10.3726/978-3-653-03807-1

© Peter Lang GmbH
Internationaler Verlag der Wissenschaften
Frankfurt am Main 2013
All rights reserved.
PL Academic Research is an Imprint of Peter Lang GmbH.
Peter Lang – Frankfurt am Main · Bern · Bruxelles · New York · Oxford · Warszawa ·
Wien

This book is part of an editor's series of PL Academic Research
and was peer reviewed prior to publication.

www.peterlang.com

Contents

Contents

CHAPTER THREE
SUSTAINABLE DEVELOPMENT IN THEORY AND APPLICATION

EDITORIAL
JÜRGEN PLÖHN
(EBC UNIVERSITY OF APPLIED SCIENCES HAMBURG/
MARTIN-LUTHER-UNIVERSITY HALLE)

The fourth volume of the series on the annual Sofia conferences is based on the meeting in 2011. Well beyond the beginning of the international financial crisis that started in 2008 and still goes on in 2013, the 2011 conference dealt with a number of continuously relevant topics, but shows a hightened interest in pressing economic problems which are related to the US-dollar, the euro and other currencies.

The first chapter of the volume in hand consists of articles that are related in one way or another to currency problems and to the underlying economic crisis.

In a thoughtful article Corbett Gaulden addresses fiscal aspects of the European debt crisis from an American perspective, i.e. from the outside. He is especially interested in the relationship between short-term social welfare and long term fiscal policy. Thus Gaulden links the economic problems to politicians as policy makers.

George Chobanov and Teodor Sedlarski use mathematical formula in order to express their ideas of social justice in a free society. As a superior equilibrium state can be reached by public policy rather than by pure market processes, the two Bulgarian authors strongly argue in favour of interventions into the economic process. A really human society requires more than the crude survival of the fittest, they stress.

Jean-Pierre Gern's contribution to this volume shows an even higher degree of skepticism towards neoliberal market economies. Gern points to differences between the competitiveness of states and the European Union on the one hand and individual enterprises on the other. Gern shows severe doubts in the desirability of an unrestricted growth of advertising activities and the production of goods that serve "artificial needs". Thus Gern challenges some basic assumptions of a free market based economy.

For the second chapter, three articles have been selected which are related to specific experiences in different nations and may give some direction for the further development of European nations. Luca Bartocci and Francesca Picciaia describe theoretical changes in the perception of governance, some British, US-American and Canadian experiences and policy changes in Italy. The authors advocate a consiliation between public authorities, society and the market in order to overcome the old controversy which side should have the prevalence.

A German group consisting of Christian Scheiner, Christian Baccarella, Stephan Hohenadl and Kai-Ingo Voigt contributes an analysis on the Nuremberg area in Northern Bavaria. The region's dynamic economy develops in certain clusters. But as numerous firms are relatively young, according to the empirical findings, the desired positive externalities of the clusters have still remained relatively weak.

Stefka Iankova discusses different factors mentioned in literature for the success of mergers and acquisitions. She tests several previously published hypotheses by a survey among Bulgarian enterprises. By far not all of the hypotheses can find substantial support. But similarity appears to be of major relevance.

The third chapter is devoted to a rather modern topic of economics: sustainability. Joachim Schwalbach contributes a short note on trustworthiness in economic relations. Stable social relations are seen as a precondition for a long-term and thus sustainable economic development.

Dieter Flämig addresses the topic of sustainability by referring to English and German literature. Flämig advocates a careful consideration of all external effects of production on the environment. In order to cope with the environmental challenge, he wants to integrate diverse efforts like city planning, public transportation and old age pensions into a comprehensive concept of a sustainable economy.

Andreas Scholz-Fleischmann gives a report on various methods for the treatment of organic waste in Berlin. His Berlin Waste Management and Street-Cleaning Company is heading for closed cycles in the collection, treatment and disposal of organic waste in the German capital. Scholz-Fleischmann presents this goal as corresponding to the EU strategy for Corporate Social Responsibility.

Of course, as a whole, this fourth volume of the series on the Sofia conferences shows a clear pro-market orientation. But it clings to a specific Continental European position: The authors' belief in the market is a qualified one.

CHAPTER ONE:

THEORETICAL ECONOMIC APPROACHES

FISCAL MISCHIEF AND FISCAL CONSTRAINT
IN THE EUROPEAN CRISIS

CORBETT F. GAULDEN
(ANGELO STATE UNIVERSITY, TEXAS, USA)

Introduction

Capital markets, and those of us who watch what happens on the global stage, are practically breathless as we watch the unfolding economic and fiscal drama of modern Europe. Since this paper was presented almost three months ago[1], governments have failed and regularly scheduled national elections have occurred all over Europe, both in the western and eastern economies. Greece and Italy have been at the precipice and their crises are still not fully resolved. The need to shift toward more financial austerity has come into conflict with public expectations concerning various entitlements. While the array of entitlements varies from nation to nation, the underlying phenomenon seems to be the need to meet the expectations of the national populaces and an apparent inability to pay for those from the extant public coffers.

Three days after this keynote paper was presented at the 14th Conference, the announcement of the Nobel Prize for Economics for 2011 was made. The prize was awarded to two American economists – Sargent and Sims. Their work emphasized that fiscal policy and practice impacts the general economy. This is a factor often overlooked in fiscal planning. Ignoring this fact may result in economic disaster as fiscal policies are implemented.

I am indebted to numerous sources, mostly current, for the ideas presented herein. These sources are dominated by the daily stream of news media in Europe and the USA. They are accompanied by the constantly changing stream of information found on the websites of the various nations in Europe and an array of affected funding entities. More stable elements for analysis of our very fluid situation are provided by *Anders 2010*, *Das 2010*, and *Copelovitch 2010*.

1. Welfare: Content or Method?

In the late eighteenth century, an assembly of forefathers of the United States of America wrote the following as a preamble to the constitution of the United States:

---

[1] Conference held on October 7 and 8, 2011 (the editors).

"We the people of the United States, in Order to form a more perfect Union, establish Justice, insure domestic Tranquility, provide for the common defense, *promote the general Welfare*, and secure the Blessings of Liberty to ourselves and our Posterity, do ordain and establish this Constitution for the United States of America" (emphasis added, C.F.G.).

This general statement has been used as an underlying set of principles for the government of the USA since the time of its ratification by the various states. The clause of interest to this presentation is the clause, "promote the general Welfare" found in the center of the preamble. The other three major objectives of the USA government, established by that constitution, also receive attention and debate. However, the objective or promise of welfare is the most broadly discussed. As is true with any such human endeavor, *precise definitions are very difficult to craft*. To some extent the various Articles and Amendments to the U.S. Constitution are designed to aid our thoughts in deciding what these things mean and what we can do about them – what is appropriate to achieve the goals and what is not.

In general, the concept of a "general" welfare has evolved into the more common term *"social" welfare*. Dictionaries and textbooks, when we query them as to what social welfare means, seem to focus only on the *mechanisms* for the delivery of that social welfare, whatever it is. They are *virtually silent as to the contents* of the term. Obviously, this leaves us with a large area for discussion and argumentation in the political arena. That this argument has been a very prominent one for the century should be a point on which we all agree. It can be said that the issue has been around for a very long time, but that it became prominent in what I call the *"republican"* period – the recent time frame in which most peoples of the earth have adopted some sort of republic as the state model – at least in name if not in actual form. Note that this is not being used as the name of some political party but of a very generalized form of government purported to be representative rather than to serve the purposes of some "royal" agenda. Hence, it appeals broadly to the ideas of Plato, but in the form of some centralized collective will.

1.1 Private or Public Welfare?

We certainly see in modern republics a wide variety of *de facto* approaches by the various governments to provide a definition of social (or general) welfare. To some extent, welfare is a private matter. In fact, in many economic systems, a fairly heavy emphasis is placed on what we in the US call *"private charity."* The concept of private charity is that many social needs can be, and in fact are, met through personal benevolence, which is private citizens giving to other citizens resources that are useful in providing welfare to the recipients at the personal expense of the donors. Research seems to indicate that nations are very different in the extent to which their citizens engage in such activities. Furthermore, governments seem to vary considerably in the extent to which they encourage or even acknowledge such activities.

Whatever level of interest governments show in "people helping people" directly, it appears they perceive that such a system is inadequate because of sector size or perceived "fairness" to take care of all needs of their societies. What is meant here is that governments cannot guarantee that the sizes of welfare systems are adequate to the task unless *they* decide on the size of the effort. They inherently distrust that the sector will always rise to the challenges experienced by the society. Governments purport to know better than a collective subconscious what the current scope of such needs is. They perceive that they have a social mandate (the undefined *moral imperative*) that includes an automatic understanding of these needs.

Furthermore, they believe that documents such as US Constitution explicitly require them to be involved in providing welfare. Hence, to one degree or another, governments become the *arbiters* of what social welfare is, who receives what in a social welfare system and the mechanisms that accompany such a system. A slightly cynical point of view is that governments are quite unlikely to permit the conclusion that private charity is adequate to fully care for the needs of a society because the governments cannot *control* private charity very well. Governments can, by contrast, control a government-run social welfare system. Only this, they seem to perceive, will permit them to respond explicitly to relevant constituencies. It will naturally be preferred, then, to *de facto* welfare systems.

In the absence of the perception of control, governments will concern themselves that the social needs they perceive to be important are not being adequately attended. It seems inevitable that part of the power they receive from voting constituencies will be based on the needs those constituencies perceive to be important. Hence, governments feel a strong need to steer the social welfare structure. They will seek to determine several things:

- the current definition of social welfare (contents of the system);
- who will be the recipients of the social welfare system;
- what will be the scope of that system;
- how the welfare system will be delivered, and
- how the system will be financed including the overall cost.

It is not very difficult to perceive that, in national elections in contemporary times, political parties frequently attempt to distinguish themselves from competing political parties along a fairly small number of dimensions, at least one of which is some sort of packaging of some issues that most would agree are matters of "social welfare" that are important to one or more constituencies that might support the political party in question. However, the "issue in question" might well be very differently viewed by other constituencies. The election, then, is won by the party or coalition of parties that most closely represents the current mood of some majority of the voting electorate.

De facto, the argument just presented illustrates that the various political opponents and the constituencies they represent possess different points of view about what "social welfare" actually is. That fundamental disagreement will obviously also extend to implementation of changes in "social welfare" programs by the government. The then newly current sense of that definition of "social welfare" will be different than it was before the election and it is different than it would have been if the collective electorate had chosen some other party/coalition. "Social welfare" is thus a dynamic concept. It is used by various political entities to bring about the need to shift power in an economy. The shift of power is necessary to sustain attempts at achievement of whatever agenda.

2. Social Welfare and Fiscal Policy

That, in and of itself, should be perfectly fine to us who believe in some sort of democratic society. It should also be okay to us that this phenomenon will shift with time. The difficulty for us is that changes in "social welfare" systems will invariably result in changes in fiscal policy. Unfortunately for political entities, *the economy is not immune to changes in fiscal policy*. Any shift in fiscal policy will result in perturbations to the existing economy at the time of the shifts.

In modern times, most people agree that shifts that are too radical in their nature *can* result in harm to the fiscal (economic for this discussion) system that cannot be easily overcome. When such things occur, chaos *can* ensue. The system of soviets resulted in this kind of phenomenon over time. To an outside observer, current situations in states such as Greece are largely related to an inability of statesmen to manage the fiscal policies that are required for them to *responsibly keep their promises* to some of the constituencies who put them into power. When they fail to do so, political turmoil may well be the result.

At some level, when political entities promise more than the economy can bear by way of cost support, a kind of "fiscal foolishness" or "fiscal mischief" has emerged. If the constituencies who expect the promised social benefits continue to insist on the providence of those benefits, the fiscal strain may become too much and the state may find itself unable to meet various sets of obligations. At some point this may even result in defaults on various kinds of obligations. Typically, these defaults will be targeted outwardly rather than onto the grantors of power. This, of course, creates credit problems in a world where free flow of capital is very basically necessary. The resultant drying up of access to capital then frustrates the entire economic system, and troubles can sometimes spiral out of control.

2.1 Finite Wealth Pool

A central tenet of many economic beliefs is that the supply of wealth at any point in time is finite – slightly flexible but finite. Another unspoken principle is that amassed wealth is much more effective at generating more wealth than is broadly distributed wealth. Broadly distributed wealth cannot be readily disciplined to generate more wealth. From an economic perspective, much of the wealth of any system is not used well or productively. To the extent the wealth is broadly distributed, it is feared by some, the tendency to slow wealth generation is even more pronounced. Further, nearly everyone agrees that government expenditures do not produce wealth, they use it. A conclusion is that the use of wealth by government to support the perceived (agenda-ized) social welfare is destructive to the pool of available wealth. Hence, the capacity to generate more wealth is reduced by the size of government run social welfare programs. Up to some point this must be accepted so that basic social needs are met. The extent to which this is desirable is at the point of any social welfare debate.

When a government promises a larger social welfare system than any other entity perceives to be desirable, fiscal mischief has occurred insofar as that entity (such as a competing political party) is concerned. Therefore, a political agenda that includes an aggressive social agenda will be accused of being fiscally foolish because of the impact of the expenditure requirements of the programs. Inherent increases in expenditures for the pursuit of the programs will result in deductions from the available pool of wealth for purposes that are not considered to be economically productive nor will they be evaluated on dimensions that are directly related to economic productivity.

2.2 The Crisis and Mischief

In the apparently still ongoing European Debt Crisis, some make the argument that "fiscal mischief" is, at least, one of the causes of the various messes: if not a cause, at least a contributor to the magnitude and duration of the crisis. Based on the "recovery" requirements imposed by the international banking community (for example, joint IMF and EU loans) one may assume that the nations engaged in trying to salvage the various economies believe that the governments of those economies have been fiscally foolish or, more simply, fiscally mischievous.

A prominent feature, in fact, of application to EU membership is an insistence on what the underwriting nations have set as standards for fiscal practice. Membership is highly conditioned on meeting those standards. Nations where the providence of social welfare utilizes a high proportion of GDP find it more difficult to meet the requirements, as the likelihood of meeting other domestic and international obligations diminishes generally with more emphasis on social welfare expenditures.

The states of eastern Europe, which emerged from the soviet system some two decades ago, had existed for forty to seventy years in an economic system that carried the promise that virtually every personal economic concern was a matter for social welfare programming. When that extremely strongly entrenched system collapsed economically, the states went immediately from almost total social welfare to whatever else could be devised. The repressive nature of the soviet system led the emerging peoples to a large attraction to capitalism. Along with that attraction came a desire to become affiliated with western institutions such as the EU. Rejection of the system of the soviets coupled with a desire to gain access to western capital markets apparently contributed to two major phenomena. One was an immediate movement toward more conservative forms of government and the other was a need to reform, among other things, fiscal policy into a more conservative format.

Fiscal conservatism, or more accurately the shift toward fiscal conservatism, has not been without difficulty. While the economies in question have adopted fiscal policies that were required by western lending entities, the loss in customary social services has sometimes resulted in political backlash. As a result a certain "back-and-forth" phenomenon is often seen in national elections. The peoples have attempted to move forward economically but innately remember when the state "took care" of everything.

2.3 Fiscal Conservatism

It is a simple fact that an economy cannot develop as quickly as a government can change or a fiscal policy can be enacted. The resultant disharmony of outcomes causes some measure of social stress, which is manifested in future election results. In other words, the cycle and pace of political changes may exceed the capacity of the economic system for matching change. The simple magnitude of the required changes may be impossible to achieve in any short run, even when the national consciousness approves of the political goals.

The apparent solution to the high-amplitude cycles just discussed is to diminish the rate of change in either direction (conservative or liberal shifts) so that the economy can keep pace with the changes. As mentioned however, political elections are practically instantaneous events (compared to the pace of change which an economy can successfully endure) and can throw everything out of balance quite quickly. The odd factor in this equation is access to capital markets. The capital markets of eastern Europe seem to have been mostly depleted by the end of the soviet economic collapse. Capital to rebuild and save shattered systems had to be sought outside the boundaries of that exhausted system. Hence, the clear need for access to extra-regional capital supplies (more simply, portable wealth) emerged immediately. This led to competing sets of fiscal expectations: those of a citizenry completely adapted to state supported welfare systems and those of the necessary wealth sources. The required compromises between the expectations of continued state providence and the demands for more moderate fiscal policy on the part of lending states is a matter requiring great diplomatic skill.

Another reality is that the globalization of wealth is, in and of itself, cyclical. Fortunately, in recent times, the degree of globalization of wealth has been fairly high. The fluidity of wealth is at least partially a function of the expectation of returns to the use of the wealth. In other words, lenders currently have a high tolerance for international lending in exchange for acceptable returns.

3. Fiscal Balance

However, the *moral imperative* of aiding weaker economies must be balanced against possible economic returns for doing so. Members of the G5, for example, seem to be quite willing to aid in various regions of the world but are not under legal compunction to do so. Intra-European lending has been fairly popular in the post-soviet era. However willing the lenders may be however, they generally want to hedge current loan success against future economic well-being to the emerging states. This hedge takes the form of various requirements for aid. Many of those requirements translate into fiscal reforms. Most entities that are interested in such guarantees for the safekeeping of entrusted wealth would state that this is simple fiscal prudence or "fiscal constraint." The emerging states are obligated to meet some such terms in order to obtain the appropriate financing for their economies to emerge. These loan (or aid) terms may be incompatible with existing structures for social welfare. This produces the social/political struggle that leads to election shifts.

The demand for social services to which a people are accustomed finds itself in conflict with the demands of those who control access to the wealth needed for an economy to emerge. The central argument of this presentation is that fiscal constraint will promote long-term growth. When these conditions prevail, social welfare is maximized in the long-term while fiscal health is maintained for the state. At the other end of the argument is the proposition that short-term, politically popular programs often result in fiscal mischief and long-term decline in social welfare. The central question is where to find the balance between an insatiable need for more social welfare in the short run and long run economic health. The soviet experience shows us that simply seizing all available wealth to increase the scope of the welfare state will soon exhaust the wealth and result in political repression. Having seized virtually all the available wealth and alienated itself from the rest of the world by failing to be a good business partner, the soviet system had to resort to repression to maintain control and prevent lawlessness.

It is not unfair to assert that the European debt crisis is not actually over yet. At the same time, it is fair to argue that some of the affected states recovered quite well from the initial problems and that their fiscal conservatism continues to serve them well economically, however much political angst there may be. There were a wide variety of aid packages and some unusual collaborative aid efforts involved in the early activities directed at coping with the crisis. These appear likely to persist into the rest of the debt crisis *if the wealth holds out.* However, as the crisis has spread to the rest of Europe and to the remaining G5 nations, the aid packages may not be as available, simply because the wealth is already reduced. This should manifest itself in more demanding fiscal requirements, which may well result in more social discontent with those policies. And the cycle might continue, but on a downward spiral, as the available wealth is further exhausted.

Furthermore, the available wealth has even more demands on it now than it did three years ago when the crisis arguably began. In fact, more demand for wealth to solve domestic problems seems to be emerging. This shift is a difficult one to manage because there is no external entity to place requirements on the use of the wealth. In the wealthier (lender) nations, the same tension between social welfare and fiscal health is also at work, even though the social welfare programs are further along in their development. Domestic needs may begin to cause a retrenchment of capital available to aid economic development in the weaker economies. This is a manifestation of the phenomenon of "isolationism" under whatever banner.

4. "Lender" Variation

At the same time, some international organizations have a keener interest in ideas that fall into the "social welfare" camp. Typically, such organizations are less interested in the financing of economies than they are in some particular social issue. They may even encourage holders of wealth to engage in development projects that have short-term social goals as a higher priority than long-term goals. Such projects might even appear to run counter to the goals of institutions whose activities are more economic in nature. Without commenting on the value of such programs, they can quite well add to the matrix of competing political forces. They might even become outside forces impacting domestic policy. The result of these forces in the world might look like pressure in the direction of political mischief in some circles, thus adding to the political and economic complexity of solutions to fiscal problems on the one hand and social problems on the other.

Simply reading the goals of various potential lending institutions will lead one to the conclusion that the various entities actually have different goals in mind when they are considering requests for aid. For example, the World Bank and the International Monetary Fund are two entities that lend with very different requirements imposed on the borrowers. It is not our purpose to evaluate the various goals but to point out that they exist. The variances suggest that borrowers might well shop their needs consistent with their own fiscal expectations as derived from their own political realities. This phenomenon will add considerable complexity to the discussion of fiscal policy.

The rich matrix of variation in national policy of borrowing nations and the policies of lending entities may well bewilder the observer. What one lending entity may view as very foolish policy on the part of a particular borrower may well be quite appealing to another lending entity. Simple declarations regarding what is appropriate in fiscal policy, then, are a function of who are the parties to the potential lending relationship.

However, recent history during the European crisis indicates a strong tendency toward the requirement for more fiscally conservative policies. This, in turn, seems to be paying off in the ability of the borrowing economies to endure the hard times and recover economically.

The question remains that how a particular lending entity approaches its relationship with a borrowing entity is highly individualized to the particular situation. The borrower response will result in changes, some of which will directly affect the existing set of expectations regarding the needs of the people in the borrower nation. In particular, social expenditures become a target for change, which may result in significant resistance that might even affect the actual ability to acquire aid. A perhaps naïve approach to untying the resultant Gordian knot could start with actually specifying the entire array of desirable characteristics for social welfare systems and then considering the fiscal methods in advance for achieving those unmet goals. It is true that the specification of the social welfare goals would evolve over time, but if an agreed upon program for achieving social welfare goals while not engaging in fiscal mischief could begin to prevail in political circles, the rancor of political entities could be reduced. Subsequently, orderly progress toward mutually acceptable goals could be maintained without threatening the pool of wealth. The pool of wealth must be maintained to sustain the attainment of future economic and social goals.

5. Conclusions

The difficult tri-partite phenomenon (fiscal policy makers, the general public and pools of available wealth) almost never works in perfect harmony. Policy makers (politicians) both stir up and work to provide social programs in order to acquire or maintain power. These policy makers must then go to the wealth pool in the short run in order to provide what has been promised. The consequence is, at best, a short-term shock to the economic system. When the shock is too large, there is a danger of a very slow recovery from the shock which retards the replenishment (or enlargement) of the wealth pool. This makes the future providence of new social welfare programs more problematic.

The absence of open dialogue makes these problems much difficult to solve. And, in fact, it may be in the best interest of policy makers to avoid holding an open discussion with the voting public. Such a discussion cannot be easily reduced to political slogans. Furthermore, the voting public will normally take a fairly short-term view of its own welfare.

If there were a dialogue, it would need to focus on the trade-off between short-term welfare decisions and long-term decisions. That solution to that conflict continues to elude policy makers who continue to control whether the dialogue will be held or not.

References

Aslund, Anders: "The Last Shall be the First," Peterson Institute for International Economics, Washington, DC, October 2010.
Copelovitch, Mark S.: "The International Monetary Fund in the Global Economy," Cambridge University Press, Cambridge 2010.
Das, Dilip K.: "Financial Globalization: Growth, Integration, Innovation and Crisis," Palgrave MacMillan, Houndmills, Basingstoke, Hampshire 2010.

ON THE ECONOMIC POLICY DILEMMA: ECONOMIC DARWINISM VERSUS INTERVENTIONISM

GEORGE CHOBANOV / TEODOR SEDLARSKI
(SOFIA UNIVERSITY "ST. KLIMENT OHRIDSKI", BULGARIA)

Help survive, or let the market do its job –
that is the question of economic policy choice.

1. Basic goals of economic policy

Economic policy's *ideal* is the achievement of welfare for everyone, meaning the satisfaction of needs of every member of the society to the degree desired by him. This ideal is an unachievable goal that humanity is striving for, trying to approximate it through the creation of an effective economic system. It is not accidental, that some of the fundamental economic monographs are devoted to the welfare of all members of society, e.g. 'Welfare for All' by Ludwig Erhard (Erhard 1957) or the 'Wealth of Nations' by Adam Smith (Smith 1776).

The goal or *goals* that an economic policy can have come down to the achieving of the ideal: welfare for all and more precisely the satisfaction of all citizens' needs. In order for the people's needs to be satisfied with material and intellectual goods the latter have to be produced, distributed and consumed. For the goods to be distributed and consumed they have to exist, i.e. to be first produced. That is why the satisfaction with goods depends primarily but not only on the production capacity of the economic system. In most cases that is meant by the expression "a nation's economy". The production capacity of an economy is the quantity of all goods and services that can be produced in a given period of time with all disposable means of production. The quantity of actually produced goods within an economy over a certain period of time (usually a year) is measured by the Gross Domestic Product.

As the availability of more goods leads potentially to more satisfied needs, it is a natural aim to expand the production. As the classical definition states, economic growth is the quantitative increase of the real GDP of a nation's economy in a given period of time. Economic growth can be the increase of GDP of an economy functioning under its potential capacity (production possibilities curve) without any change in this potential capacity. If the economy functions with its full potential, than the only way for it to grow is to increase its production possibilities frontier, i.e. the means of production. That is why in the long run economic growth means the increase of the production capacity of an economy.

The *first main goal* of economic policy is to stimulate balanced growth i.e. a linear trend of increase, a constant speed of growth. The aim of the balanced growth is to compensate for the phases of economic cycles, to reduce their amplitude through a so called counter cyclical economic (fiscal) policy which tempers the abrupt growth or decline of the economic activity. What the pace of growth of an economy should be is hard to prescribe as for the developed countries, where the economic system usually functions at its full capacity, like for example Germany, 1 per cent p.a. is a normal growth rate and 2 per cent is high. In less developed countries like Bulgaria or China which have to catch up, a 5 per cent growth could be described as "normal" while, for example, "high" is 7-10 per cent p.a. Taken as a whole, it would be desirable for the world economy to increase by 1-2 per cent p.a. Economic growth cannot be limitless because it depletes Earth's resources and pollutes the environment. The industrial revolution, which was the cause of an unseen economic growth, has in the same time led to depletion of the natural resources to an extent that threatens the existence of the human race. This fact was realized by the world's community by the mid of the 20th century and has found a place in the report "Limits of Growth", published in 1972 by the Club of Rome (Paschke 2001: 204). In this and other publications by the Club of Rome the negative consequences of growth are considered and the idea of humanity's responsibility is defended not only for the ecosystem, but also for the social environment, the responsibility of every human generation for the next and the human kind as a whole. This responsibility is synthesized in the concept of *sustainable development*. It means that in the production of goods only as many resources may be used as can be substituted by new ones.

The increase of the production capacity depends directly on the propensity of the enterprises to invest in means of production. The enterprises would widen their production capacity, and thus the supply of goods, if they expect to be able to sell the produced goods. Hence economic growth depends directly on the supply and its determinants and indirectly on the demand. These dependencies suggest the possible approaches for realizing an economic policy toward economic growth: the demand approach and the supply approach. The demand for goods depends not only on the prices, but also on the solvency of the demanding subjects, usually the households, which on its part is determined to a great extent by their income, i.e. the general level of employment.

The achievement of full employment is economic policy's *second main goal*. Full employment means that a job is available to everyone who wishes to work and the unemployment is zero. This condition is achieved very rarely and is even considered practically almost impossible. An unemployment level of 2-3 per cent is considered by economists to be full employment.

The purchasing power of the economic agents' incomes depends on the price level. The objective of a constant price level or a low inflation is the *third main goal* of the economic policy or more precisely of the monetary policy. The price level is considered stable if within a year the inflation doesn't exceed 2 per cent.

For the need of everyone or almost everyone in the society to be satisfied it is not enough to produce a lot of goods. It is also necessary that a just system for income distribution functions in the economy. The problem of social justice is as old as humanity itself. It consists of two main questions:

I. Which distribution is just?

II. How should a just income distribution be achieved?

The *fourth main goal* of the economic policy is the achievement of social justice, which brings economic policy close to social policy. The four goals are crucial to the conduct of an economic policy within a closed economy. As modern economies are open ones, another goal has to be added: The maintenance of an equilibrium in the exchange with the rest of the world is the *fifth main goal* of the economic policy (for the whole discussion see introductory literature, for example, Beeker 2011; Klump 2011; Mussel/Pätzold 2012; Wildmann 2012).

2. Economic equilibrium

The economy as organism – like every other dynamic system – constantly passes from one state to another, some of which are equilibrium ones and others non-equilibrium states. Which system state can we call an "equilibrium"? What does "equilibrium" mean? It is a question which leads us to the genesis of the existence of things in the world we live in.

The ancient Chinese philosophers noted that everything exists because of the equilibrated unity of two opposites – the two sides of its nature. In economics, the two opposites that determine the nature of the market are the demand and supply. Equilibrating the market (reaching the equilibrium) is a result of the satisfaction of opposite interests to a desired degree by both opposing sides. The opposing interests can be brought to balance not only within a market. The economic system is a complex conglomerate of relationships and opposites, which need to be in balance if the system shall exist normally and in coordination as a whole, living organism. Over time it goes in and out of equilibrium.

A stable system, when out of equilibrium, returns to the initial or some other equilibrium state by itself. In this case we say that the system is

self-regulating, and the equilibrium states, to which the system returns automatically, are called stable equilibrium states.
An example of a stable equilibrium state is the walking man: When he is making a step, he is transitioning from an equilibrium to a disequilibrium state and then again to another equilibrium state. If a man wants to stay in one place without moving he is constantly in the same stable equilibrium state. But if he wants to move to a further location he will have to leave the equilibrium and enter some disequilibrium state in order the reach another equilibrium state.

The development of an economic system is impossible without exiting from equilibrium into disequilibrium and then the transition to another equilibrium state.

The analysis of the dynamics of the economic system – much like in mathematical physics – dates back to the early neoclassical school (Walras [1926] 1954; Marshall, [1890] 1920). Its contemporary form started to appear in the 1930s, mainly in the discussions of renown econometricians like the Nobel prize winners Frisch (1936) and Tinbergen (1935) as well as in the works of Samuelson (1947; cf. Gandolfo 1997) and was then integrated into the so called 'neoclassical synthesis'. This concept led to the development of the theories of comparative statics and dynamics (Samuelson 1947). Nowadays the comparative statics and dynamics are the methodological basis of the research of a great number of modern economists (cf. Boulding 1971; Gandolfo 1997).

The economic variables which determine the states of an economic system are endogenous or exogenous. *Exogenous or external variables*, denoted by $\alpha_1, \alpha_2, ..., \alpha_m$, specify the conditions under which an economic system is functioning. Endogenous or internal variables, denoted by $x_1, x_2, ..., x_n$, get their values as a result of internal relationships in the economic system under the conditions of the external environment, determined by the values of exogenous variables. A state ω in a certain moment of time is therefore expressed by a vector $\omega = (x_1, x_2, ..., x_n, \alpha_1, \alpha_2, ..., \alpha_m)$ involving all the exogenous variables $\alpha_1, \alpha_2, ..., \alpha_m$ and endogenous variables $x_1, x_2, ..., x_n$.

Exogenous and endogenous variables or parameters in an economic system are specified by its structure and regulations. Under some conditions a parameter of an economic system could be exogenous, under other conditions, the same parameter could become endogenous. For example, under currency board conditions an exchange rate has to be fixed with respect to another currency, therefore being set to be an exogenous parameter. A floating exchange rate is determined by a supply-demand relationship and, therefore, has to be considered as an endogenous parameter.

In a national economy all parameters set up by government, like tax and insurance levels or the overall government budget macro-frame, are externally given by regulations and, therefore, are to be considered as exogenous. Given values of exogenous parameters, endogenous parameters are the result of relationships within the economic system. *Thus, endogenous parameters are functions of exogenous parameters*, like

$$x_1 = x_1(\alpha_1, \alpha_2, ..., \alpha_m)$$
$$x_2 = x_2(\alpha_1, \alpha_2, ..., \alpha_m)$$

$$x_n = x_n(\alpha_1, \alpha_2, ..., \alpha_n)$$

Since we consider dynamic systems, the state ω of the system depends on time t, which means that $\omega = (x_1, x_2, ..., x_n, \alpha_1, \alpha_2, ..., \alpha_m)$ is a function of t: $\omega(t) = (x_1(t), x_2(t), ..., x_n(t), \alpha_1, \alpha_2, ..., \alpha_m)$.

Endogenous parameters $(x_1, x_2, ..., x_n)$ change with time t and exogenous parameters are considered to stay relatively constant. In certain moments or periods of time exogenous parameters could change quite drastically as well, which changes the conditions for the functioning of the whole economic system. An essential change in an exogenous parameter is called a *shock*.

The relationships determining the states of the system $\omega(t)$ in every moment of time t could be expressed by functional simultaneous equations:

$$f_1(x_1(t), x_2(t), ..., x_n(t), \alpha_1, \alpha_2, ..., \alpha_m) = 0$$
$$f_2(x_1(t), x_2(t), ..., x_n(t), \alpha_1, \alpha_2, ..., \alpha_m) = 0$$
$$...$$
$$f_n(x_1(t), x_2(t), ..., x_n(t), \alpha_1, \alpha_2, ..., \alpha_m) = 0$$

(1)

given the state $(x_1(0), x_2(0), ..., x_n(0)) = (x_1^0, x_2^0, ..., x_n^0)$ in the initial moment of time $t = 0$ and functions $f_1, f_2, ..., f_n$, describing the relationships in the economic system.

Functional simultaneous equations (1) could be any kind of functional equations, but most often dynamics is represented by a parameter's velocity or speed of change

$$(\dot{x}_1, \dot{x}_2, ..., \dot{x}_n) = (\frac{dx_1}{dt}, \frac{dx_2}{dt}, ..., \frac{dx_n}{dt})$$ of state $(x_1, x_2, ..., x_n)$. Usually:

$$\dot{x}_1 = g_1(f_1(x_1(t), x_2(t), ..., x_n(t), \alpha_1, \alpha_2, ..., \alpha_m))$$
$$\dot{x}_2 = g_2(f_2(x_1(t), x_2(t), ..., x_n(t), \alpha_1, \alpha_2, ..., \alpha_m))$$
$$...$$
$$\dot{x}_n = g_n(f_n(x_1(t), x_2(t), ..., x_n(t), \alpha_1, \alpha_2, ..., \alpha_m)) \qquad (2)$$

given functions $(g_1, g_2, ..., g_n)$ with: $g_i(-z) = -g_i(z)$ and $g_i(0) = 0$, for $i = 1, 2, ..., n$ and for every z. Particularly, functions $(g_1, g_2, ..., g_n)$ could be equal to any constants $(k_1, k_2, ..., k_n)$:

$$g_i = k_i, \ i = 1, 2, ..., n,$$

In this particular case (1) becomes:

$$\dot{x}_1 = k_1 f_1(x_1(t), x_2(t), ..., x_n(t), \alpha_1, \alpha_2, ..., \alpha_m)$$
$$\dot{x}_2 = k_2 f_2(x_1(t), x_2(t), ..., x_n(t), \alpha_1, \alpha_2, ..., \alpha_m)$$
$$...$$
$$\dot{x}_n = k_n f_n(x_1(t), x_2(t), ..., x_n(t), \alpha_1, \alpha_2, ..., \alpha_m), \qquad (3)$$

The endogenous parameter state $(\bar{x}_1, \bar{x}_2, ..., \bar{x}_n)$ is said to be a ***dynamic equilibrium state***, if t satisfies (1) for all admissible moments of time t:

$$f_1(\bar{x}_1, \bar{x}_2, ..., \bar{x}_n, \alpha_1, \alpha_2, ..., \alpha_m) = 0$$
$$f_2(\bar{x}_1, \bar{x}_2, ..., \bar{x}_n, \alpha_1, \alpha_2, ..., \alpha_m) = 0$$
$$...$$
$$f_n(\bar{x}_1, \bar{x}_2, ..., \bar{x}_n, \alpha_1, \alpha_2, ..., \alpha_m) = 0 \qquad (4)$$

which means that $(x_1(t), x_2(t), ..., x_n(t)) = (\bar{x}_1, \bar{x}_2, ..., \bar{x}_n)$, for every t, is a solution of the functional simultaneous equations (3).

The dynamic equilibrium state $(\bar{x}_1, \bar{x}_2, ..., \bar{x}_n)$ satisfies (2):

$$0 = \dot{\bar{x}}_1 = g_1(f_1(\bar{x}_1(t), \bar{x}_2(t), ..., \bar{x}_n(t), \alpha_1, \alpha_2, ..., \alpha_m)) = 0$$
$$0 = \dot{\bar{x}}_2 = g_2(f_2(\bar{x}_1(t), \bar{x}_2(t), ..., \bar{x}_n(t), \alpha_1, \alpha_2, ..., \alpha_m)) = 0$$
$$...$$
$$0 = \dot{\bar{x}}_n = g_n(f_n(\bar{x}_1(t), \bar{x}_2(t), ..., \bar{x}_n(t), \alpha_1, \alpha_2, ..., \alpha_m)) = 0,$$

since $(\dot{\bar{x}}_1, \dot{\bar{x}}_2, ..., \dot{\bar{x}}_n) = (0, 0, ..., 0)$ and $g_i(0) = 0$, for $i = 1, 2, ..., n$.

The equilibrium states of a dynamic economic system could be stable or unstable. Since stability could reduce uncertainty a lot of efforts were devoted to the investigation of the economic system's stable states and self-regulating mechanisms directing it automatically to an equilibrium state (cf. Marshall 1879; 1890; Walras [1926] 1954; Gandolfo 1997).

Comparative statics is concerned with an equilibrium analysis of the economic system, based on partial derivatives $\dfrac{\partial x_i}{\partial \alpha_j}$, $i = 1,2,...,n$, $j = 1,2,...,m$. It seeks to determine only the direction of change of the variables, but not whether the system returns to an equilibrium state since the latter is a matter of *comparative dynamics*.

The methodology in comparative statics and dynamics is based on Samuelson's *correspondence principle*, which states that first the statics has to be investigated and then the corresponding dynamics.

The comparative statics method was used by Slutsky ([1915] 1953), Hicks (1939) and in a generalized form by Samuelson (1947).

As it has already been shown, any equilibrium state of the economic system can be represented as a solution of the simultaneous equations:

$$f_1(x_1,x_2,...,x_n,\alpha_1,\alpha_2,...,\alpha_m) = 0$$
$$f_2(x_1,x_2,...,x_n,\alpha_1,\alpha_2,...,\alpha_m) = 0$$
$$...$$
$$f_n(x_1,x_2,...,x_n,\alpha_1,\alpha_2,...,\alpha_m) = 0$$

where $f_1, f_2,...,f_n$ are functions of $n+m$ variables, which we can solve under certain conditions, if we express the endogenous variables $x_1,x_2,...,x_n$ through the exogenous variables $\alpha_1,\alpha_2,...,\alpha_m$, thus finding the equilibrium values

$$x_1 = x_1(\alpha_1,\alpha_2,...,\alpha_m)$$
$$x_2 = x_2(\alpha_1,\alpha_2,...,\alpha_m)$$
$$...$$
$$x_n = x_n(\alpha_1,\alpha_2,...,\alpha_m)$$

of the endogenous variables as functions of exogenous parameters $\alpha_1,\alpha_2,...,\alpha_m$, which in the neighborhood $N = N(x_1^0,x_2^0,...,x_m^0,\alpha_1^0,\alpha_2^0,...,\alpha_m^0)$ of the point $(x_1^0,x_2^0,...,x_m^0,\alpha_1^0,\alpha_2^0,...,\alpha_m^0)$ satisfy the simultaneous equations:

$$f_1(x_1(\alpha_1,\alpha_2,...,\alpha_m),x_2(\alpha_1,\alpha_2,...,\alpha_m),x_n(\alpha_1,\alpha_2,...,\alpha_m),\alpha_1,\alpha_2,...,\alpha_m) = 0$$

$$f_2(x_1(\alpha_1,\alpha_2,...,\alpha_m),x_2(\alpha_1,\alpha_2,...,\alpha_m),x_n(\alpha_1,\alpha_2,...,\alpha_m),\alpha_1,\alpha_2,...,\alpha_m) = 0$$

$$...$$
(5)

$$f_n(x_1(\alpha_1,\alpha_2,...,\alpha_m),x_2(\alpha_1,\alpha_2,...,\alpha_m),x_n(\alpha_1,\alpha_2,...,\alpha_m),\alpha_1,\alpha_2,...,\alpha_m) = 0$$

An infinitely small change in the exogenous parameter α_j, $j=1,2,...,m$, mathematically expressed with its differential $d\alpha_j$, could implicate (infinitely small) change in the endogenous parameter x_i, mathematically expressed by dx_i, $i=1,2,...,n$. The relationship between the changes dx_i and $d\alpha_j$ is given by the partial derivative $\dfrac{\partial x_i}{\partial \alpha_j}$, $i=1,2,...,n$, $j=1,2,...,m$.

Comparative statics basically investigates partial derivatives $\dfrac{\partial x_i}{\partial \alpha_j}$, $i=1,2,...,n$, $j=1,2,...,m$, in order to determine the *direction and rate of change*. In order to determine how the endogenous parameters $x_1, x_2,...,x_n$ would change if the exogenous parameter α_j is changing, we will differentiate with respect to α_j every one of equations (1):

$$\frac{\partial f_1}{\partial x_1}\frac{\partial x_1}{\partial \alpha_j}+\frac{\partial f_1}{\partial x_2}\frac{\partial x_2}{\partial \alpha_j}+...+\frac{\partial f_1}{\partial x_n}\frac{\partial x_n}{\partial \alpha_j}+\frac{\partial f_1}{\partial \alpha_j}=0$$

$$\frac{\partial f_2}{\partial x_1}\frac{\partial x_1}{\partial \alpha_j}+\frac{\partial f_2}{\partial x_2}\frac{\partial x_2}{\partial \alpha_j}+...+\frac{\partial f_2}{\partial x_n}\frac{\partial x_n}{\partial \alpha_j}+\frac{\partial f_2}{\partial \alpha_j}=0$$

...

$$\frac{\partial f_n}{\partial x_1}\frac{\partial x_1}{\partial \alpha_j}+\frac{\partial f_n}{\partial x_2}\frac{\partial x_2}{\partial \alpha_j}+...+\frac{\partial f_n}{\partial x_n}\frac{\partial x_n}{\partial \alpha_j}+\frac{\partial f_n}{\partial \alpha_j}=0$$

The latter being equivalent to following:

$$\frac{\partial f_1}{\partial x_1}\frac{\partial x_1}{\partial \alpha_j}+\frac{\partial f_1}{\partial x_2}\frac{\partial x_2}{\partial \alpha_j}+...+\frac{\partial f_1}{\partial x_n}\frac{\partial x_n}{\partial \alpha_j}=-\frac{\partial f_1}{\partial \alpha_j}$$

$$\frac{\partial f_2}{\partial x_1}\frac{\partial x_1}{\partial \alpha_j}+\frac{\partial f_2}{\partial x_2}\frac{\partial x_2}{\partial \alpha_j}+...+\frac{\partial f_2}{\partial x_n}\frac{\partial x_n}{\partial \alpha_j}=-\frac{\partial f_2}{\partial \alpha_j}$$

... $\qquad\qquad\qquad\qquad\qquad\qquad\qquad\qquad$ (6)

$$\frac{\partial f_n}{\partial x_1}\frac{\partial x_1}{\partial \alpha_j}+\frac{\partial f_n}{\partial x_2}\frac{\partial x_2}{\partial \alpha_j}+...+\frac{\partial f_n}{\partial x_n}\frac{\partial x_n}{\partial \alpha_j}=-\frac{\partial f_n}{\partial \alpha_j}$$

Solving the latter linear simultaneous equations with respect to unknown $\dfrac{\partial x_i}{\partial \alpha_j}$, $i=1,2,...,n$ we have:

$$\frac{\partial x_i}{\partial \alpha_j} = \frac{\Delta_i}{\Delta}, \ i = 1,2,\ldots,n,$$ (7)

with

$$\Delta = \begin{bmatrix} \dfrac{\partial f_1}{\partial x_1} & \dfrac{\partial f_1}{\partial x_2} & \cdots & \dfrac{\partial f_1}{\partial x_n} \\[2mm] \dfrac{\partial f_2}{\partial x_1} & \dfrac{\partial f_2}{\partial x_2} & \cdots & \dfrac{\partial f_2}{\partial x_n} \\[2mm] \cdots & & & \\[2mm] \dfrac{\partial f_n}{\partial x_1} & \dfrac{\partial f_n}{\partial x_2} & \cdots & \dfrac{\partial f_n}{\partial x_n} \end{bmatrix},$$ (8)

and Δ_i is a matrix we get from Δ by replacing

column $\begin{bmatrix} \dfrac{\partial f_1}{\partial x_i} \\[2mm] \dfrac{\partial f_2}{\partial x_i} \\[2mm] \cdots \\[2mm] \dfrac{\partial f_n}{\partial x_i} \end{bmatrix}$ in Δ by column $\begin{bmatrix} -\dfrac{\partial f_1}{\partial \alpha_j} \\[2mm] -\dfrac{\partial f_2}{\partial \alpha_j} \\[2mm] \cdots \\[2mm] -\dfrac{\partial f_n}{\partial \alpha_j} \end{bmatrix}$.

The partial derivative $\dfrac{\partial x_i}{\partial \alpha_j} = \dfrac{\Delta_i}{\Delta}$ shows how the endogenous parameter

x_i changes if the endogenous parameter α_j is altered. If $\dfrac{\partial x_i}{\partial \alpha_j} = \dfrac{\Delta_i}{\Delta} > 0$, then

x_i is an increasing function of α_j, and if $\dfrac{\partial x_i}{\partial \alpha_j} = \dfrac{\Delta_i}{\Delta} < 0$, x_i is a decreasing

function of α_j. Since sometimes we are not able to calculate $\dfrac{\Delta_i}{\Delta}$ in an ex-

plicit form, we could determine at least the sign (+ or -) of Δ and Δ_i.

Knowing the signs of $\dfrac{\partial f_i}{\partial x_j}$ and $\dfrac{\partial f_i}{\partial \alpha_k}$ is generally not enough to determine

the signs of Δ and Δ_i. Determining the signs of Δ and Δ_i, given the signs

of $\dfrac{\partial f_i}{\partial x_j}$ and $\dfrac{\partial f_i}{\partial \alpha_k}$ is possible in some special cases. Methods for determin-

ing sign of Δ and Δ_i having only the signs of $\dfrac{\partial f_i}{\partial x_j}$ and $\dfrac{\partial f_i}{\partial \alpha_k}$ are developed

by Ritschard (1983) and Fairly, Lin (1990).

The definition of a stable dynamic state shows that, if an economic system is initially in equilibrium, it will stay in it over indefinitely long time

and cannot exit this state under the influence of its own internal mechanisms, i.e. it does not change to another state by itself. But the economic system can be pushed out of an equilibrium state by exogenous factors, i.e. external forces. A change in a given exogenous parameter $\alpha_1, \alpha_2, ..., \alpha_m$ alters significantly the circumstances in which the systems functions. This kind of change is described in economics, as already mentioned, as a shock. A shock to a national economy could be e.g. the increase of the prices of energy sources, but also a change in government spending, of the interest rates or of any macroeconomic parameter, which can be interpreted as exogenous to the system. The primal role of economic policy in light of the above is to set the values of exogenous parameters so as to achieve a *desirable* equilibrium state in case the economy has experienced a shock or in case that the previous stable equilibrium state was unsatisfactory.

3. Alternative approaches to economic policy

Economic policy refers to the actions of government that are of concern to the economic system as a whole, i.e. altering the exogenous variables which determine the economic system's state. As such it is related to macroeconomics but at the same time it is meant to affect the behavior of single economic subjects on the micro level and, as a result, it should affect and change certain tendencies in desired ways, i.e. the endogenous variables. For instance, if there is a tendency towards decreasing GDP, the government can decide to stimulate the economic activities of the citizens (the country's business units) in order to change that tendency and to increase the GDP on the macro level.

Contemporary economic theory relies mainly on two approaches towards the implementation of economic policy – one of them is neoclassical, and the other – Keynesian. The contribution of Paul Samuelson and other famous economists made it possible to develop the "neoclassical synthesis" which is based upon the Keynesians approach, but combines it with neoclassical methodology. Neoclassical synthesis takes into account the circumstances, assumptions and postulates upon which both, neoclassical and Keynesian, theories are based. According to the neoclassical economic theory the market is considered as a perfect economic mechanism which is able to distribute resources by achieving equilibrium and satisfying the preferences of all participating sides without the need of state intervention.

It can be argued that the market indeed has always been the most efficient but at the same time one of the most ruthless mechanisms for maintaining an economic system. The market is actually as effective and "cruel" as the natural selection in nature. The main principles of classical

economic theory have been developed from the Renaissance period on-
wards. That was the time when mankind turned its attention back to nature's laws and that is why these main principles have been influenced
by Francois Quesnay's physiocracy ('the rule of nature'), the vitalist
school, Antoine Augustin Cournot's work, and Darwin's theory of evolution. In nature there is neither a retired lion, nor a hospital for magpies
and there is no first aid for the wounded because the sick and old should
be left behind, so only the fit ones survive and propagate.

Simply explained, when put into a competitive environment, market
forces start to balance by reaching equilibrium as some small and weak
economic subjects are led to bankruptcy while at the same time some
strong and competitive ones continue to exist.

Natural selection is the basic mechanism regulating the cyclic changes
of an animal or a plant population. In nature one population often lives
by predation on another population, for example, a population of wolfs
predates on goats. When there is a big population of the prey, then there
would be enough food for the predators and their population will increase in time while the population of the prey will decrease. This means
on the other hand that the food for the predators will diminish and their
population will also shrink, leading later on to an increase in the goats'
population etc. This is a simple self-regulating cycle.

As a living creature, man has his own specific genetically programmed
instincts. But humans are also different from any other living creature
because they have common sense, moral, and ethical standards. These
are of crucial importance for the establishment of specific rules of behavior or norms. From a humanistic point of view, social norms (legal and
informal) should be aimed at providing the ideal of economic policy –
welfare for everyone.

According to the neoclassical idea of the market economy, only a system of competitive markets is able to guarantee welfare. A competitive
and self-regulating market is a market where economic forces are balanced and in the absence of external influences the equilibrium values of
economic variables will not change. The ideal of a market economy is to
achieve a system of competitive markets. That is why legal systems and
economic policies should be constructed in such a way that all markets
of the economic system should be either competitive or self-regulating.
Unfortunately, for the time being this legal and economic problem does
not have a proper solution. It is well known that there are plenty of markets that are failing while trying to reach equilibrium. Among the reasons is that they are neither competitive, nor self-regulating. There are
some typical examples for markets which turn to be ineffective such as
monopolistic markets, some labor markets or health care services mar-

kets. In fact, every market can fail if the main principles of its functioning are not observed.

In classical and neoclassical economic theory the most important condition for the proper functioning of the market is freedom of choice for all participants. Unlimited freedom for some economic subjects on the one hand can lead to certain restrictions for others on the other hand. For that reason, freedom of action should be restrained by the principle that everyone is free to act in a way that does not restrict other people's rights. Generally, such restrictions are to be implemented through a set of social and legal norms in a society in order for a market economy to function.

4. "Law of nature" or social action

The principle of natural selection – the survival of the fittest (the terms were coined as synonyms by Herbert Spencer and Charles Darwin in the late 19th century) – can be applied not only to the competitive goods or factor markets, but also to the 'market of norms'. The notion of the 'market of norms' envisages a competition between norms of different quality which are to be adopted by a given society for regulating various branches of collective existence. By "different quality" we mean an unequal efficacy of norms. When trying to define the term efficacy of norms (or in the new institutional parlance – *institutional efficiency*) a number problems arise in theoretical discussions. Given our earlier definition of the main goal of economic policy as to ensure an Erhardian welfare for all ("Wohlstand für alle", cf. Erhard 1957), here we will assume that a norm is efficient when it contributes to this goal at the least possible (social) cost. More concrete definitions of normative efficiency like the one inherent in the World Bank's "Doing Business" reports take into account the ease with which foreign investments are done, or workers are hired and laid off, firms registered and so on. More generally such definitions focus on the ability of a set of rules to lower *transaction costs* on given markets. The notion that efficient institutions minimize average transaction costs (as widely adopted by new institutional authors) can be compatible with our broad concept that norms should enable prosperity for all, but these two perspectives can also be seen as contradictory.

Even if we decide to apply the market paradigm to the formation of social norms themselves and accept the notion that they are being set through a "market for norms" the question arises who are the economic agents involved in it. How is the supply and demand for institutional arrangements to be understood? According to both J. Schumpeter and D. North new "rules of the game" are developed intentionally (supplied) by individuals or groups of individuals, the so called institutional entrepreneurs. These people who are in positions to influence society's rules come out with new ideas about organizing economic relationships, often 'creatively destroying' old ones. On the demand side, the new rules have to be accepted by the rest of the population. They can choose to resist the institution (if the expected costs of resistance, e.g. strikes, boycotts, unrests) are lower than their losses due to the new rule.

The introduction of social institutions that increase justice and correct undesired social developments is an example of *active economic policy* which imposes additional rules on the functioning of free markets. It can be viewed as a confirmation of Polanyi's thesis (cf. Polanyi 1997 [1944]), that markets are embedded in the social fiber, and not vice-versa.

The interpretation of such measures is the focal point of the old debate about "good" economic policy. Should policy makers strive to remove all obstacles to the functioning of the free markets and thus bring about a state close to the neoclassical world of "perfect competition" or should they do just the opposite – restrain the markets (introduce alternative solutions) in a number of areas so as to bring a social (collective) element to economic life? Economic Darwinism is based on the conviction that *in the long run* competitive markets will inevitably lead to full employment and precise remuneration to every individual's skills, diligence and devotion to success. Competition is perceived as a law of nature that should not be interfered with and that all economic misfortunes of societies stem from its abandonment in favor of other culturally rooted mechanisms for coping with economic reality (cf. Sen 1993).

Usually the collapse of Marxism and other collectivistic efforts to secure the economic needs of the society are given as examples of futile approaches to economic organization. When the individual responsibility for one's own wellbeing is diluted in the group and replaced by abstract ideas about the public prosperity where nobody's contribution can be really traced the motivation for work drops sharply. Former socialist societies – as Bulgaria's – were witnessing such a development over the five decades of planned economy. If the fear of hunger and the unlimited possibilities of personal prosperity due to one's own efforts – i.e. the "carrot and the stick" of capitalist economies – are taken away, people seem to lose interest in putting their energy in the production of goods and services.

On the other hand, the notion of the "carrot and stick" is also used by the critics of the pure market economy who argue that in an advanced stage of development – like the one of the western economies today – no one is really threatened by hunger if all available resources are distributed more evenly. People do not need to be punished with food deprivation to be brought to work. In pure market conditions – the argument goes – workers are often being forced to do something against their will by capital owners who have the power to deprive them of income. In the same vein, the consumerism of modern society that makes people desire more is, according to the opponents of free markets, nothing else than a peaceful instrument to put individuals to work – endlessly spinning the wheel of the same capitalist system, that makes inequalities bigger. Neo-classical economic theory – for the antagonists of economic Darwinism – is heavily ideologically loaded and has the main goal to serve the inter-ests of certain social groups and not welfare for all.

As mentioned above, when analyzing society, not only the natural in-stincts have to be considered, but also another factor, which distin-guishes man from animal – the human mind and the resulting free will – that is used by men to shape their co-existence. So it is completely arbi-trary to base one's argumentation on natural forces when explaining so-cial processes. The whole discussion turns out to be an ideological one: economic Darwinists are using biological metaphors to impose a given social order that some members of society (individualistically and com-petitively oriented, self-centered, and those who already had financial power) were sympathetic to.

The market system itself is a complicated institutional framework build up by rigorous rules of conduct. The rules of the market game are en-forced by the community (e.g. the state) and are most probably not ge-netically predisposed as meant by 'pure market' supporters. The func-tioning of the market may have its motor in the self-centered interests of the individuals but its borders lay where certain rules seize to exist. Peo-ple in the Third World as well as the generation that lived during the transition in the post socialist societies seem to be very well aware of that latter circumstance. So the economic conduct is – as Marx was trying to show in the 19th century – a matter of social norms that can be deliberate-ly chosen to better serve the whole society or just a powerful elite (the last argument is further developed in the works of Nobel prize laureate D. North).

The concept of *bounded rationality* now widely used in institutional and cognitive economics can also help to understand the role of government and policy makers in the functioning of the economic system. Because of the limited (and unevenly distributed) information and/or the con-strained human ability to process it (maximization-oriented) economic agents cannot reach optimal market solutions as assumed by the neoclas-sical economic theory (cf. Pelikan 2004). An example is the so called *fric-tional unemployment*. In mainstream economics it is often explained by "market imperfections". It is argued that it cannot be influenced by regu-lar (Keynesian style) macroeconomic policy and that it is about 2 or 3 per

cent on average. Actually almost any kind of unemployment can be theoretically boiled down to frictions in the functioning of markets. The
slow or impeded reaction of markets towards neoclassical full employment equilibrium states is the all-encompassing explanation for unemployment, widely held in traditional economic discourses. Different lines
of argumentation point out different reasons for the markets not reaching equilibrium with full employment: from the Keynesian rigidity of
prices (e.g. monopoly explanation, cf. Kaldor 1956) to institutional design
inefficiencies. The latter are common ground for the modern strains in
economic thought as the new institutional economics and the economic
analysis of law. As information but also cognitive processing abilities are
unevenly distributed among economic agents and the governing elite,
some institutions can last for long periods of time even when there are
more efficient solutions to certain social problems (cf. Pelikan 2004).

Another argument in favor of a more activist economic policy – often
connected to the tradition of Keynesian economic thought – is that stable
market equilibriums with unwanted features (e.g. high unemployment)
are as possible and in some cases even more probable as the all-good
ones pictured by the neoclassical theorists. Assuming that markets are
not the flawless mechanisms known from traditional economic reasoning means that eventually there are certain values or normative criteria
for the desired states of the world that can supplement "market laws".
For example, people in a certain community (city district) would have
less criminality than in a "natural" (market) state or more social security
or higher employment as brought about by the market forces in a given
moment. But that would mean that the free market and unbound competition are not an all-encompassing principle in organizing social interrelations. They are merely an instrument for solving *some* economic issues
(i.e. in situations with scarce resources) that is *chosen* by the society and
that can always be supplemented by active economic policy if results are
not satisfactory. Here lies the core argument in the dispute between radical and moderate free-market-supporters: Is the market a natural or social (humanly constructed) phenomenon? If the latter is the case then the
question arises where it is productive to *choose to apply* the market mechanisms and where it should be substituted by social intervention. Real
social policy as a form of collective action toward desired social goals is
inevitably based on this latter assumption. Otherwise there would be no
need of any action, except for just "freeing the market".

5. Conclusion

In this article we have discussed the need of active social and economic
policy that corrects the mechanical functioning of markets. As opposed

to economic Darwinism, active economic policy interferes with the principles of "natural selection" in social and economic processes. The first channel through which communities i.e. governments exercise influence on the economic system is the setting of the exogenous parameters (external variables) which determine its equilibrium states. Thus economic policy contributes to balanced economic growth, tempering external shocks or helping the economic system to a transition from an undesired stable equilibrium state to a superior equilibrium state, which the system cannot reach by itself. Another channel of influence is the direct involvement in the market of social and legal norms (formal and informal institutions). Imposing rules of behavior that foster social justice and that would not have arisen under the competitive market conditions is just an example of the fundamental role of collective action in organizing social conduct. In the last two decades of the 20th century government intervention in markets and reliance on legal regulations seem to have fallen out of favour in the emerging orthodoxy of economic liberalization and Darwinian market self-selection. As the economic crisis of 2008-2011 and the continuing economic turbulences show, efforts to embed the markets back into the social context, from which they were largely freed, need to take new forms and a new scale if economic policy shall be able to succeed with fulfilling its main goals: securing welfare for the larger part of the economic subjects.

References

Beeker, D. (2011), Wirtschaftspolitik. Kompakt und praxisorientiert, Stuttgart: Kohlhammer

Boulding, K.E. (1971), "After Samuelson Who Needs Adam Smith?", in: History of Political Economy, 3, pp. 225-237.

Erhard, L. (1957), Wohlstand für alle, Düsseldorf: ECON Verlag.

Fairly, A. M. and K.-P. Lin (1990), "Qualitative Reasoning in Economics", Journal of Economic Dynamics and Control, 14, pp. 465-490.

Frisch, R. (1936), "On the Notion of Equilibrium and Disequilibrium". Review of Economic Studies, III, 1936, pp. 100-105.

Gandolfo, G. (1997), Economic Dynamics, 3rd edition, Berlin/Heidelberg: Springer.

Hicks, J. R. (1939), Value and Capital. Oxford: Clarendon Press.

Kaldor, N. (1956), "Alternative Theories of Distribution", The Review of Economic Studies, Vol. 23, 2 (1955-1956), pp. 83-100.

Klump, R. (2011), Wirtschaftspolitik. Instrumente, Ziele und Institutionen, 2nd ed. München: Pearson Studium

Marshall, A. (1879), The Pure theory of foreign trade, the pure theory of domestic values, London (Reprint 1930, London: Univ.).

Marshall, A. ([1890] 1920), Principles of Economics. 8th edition, London: Kendall, M. G.

Mussel, G. and J. Petzold (2012), Grundfragen der Wirtschaftspolitik, 8th ed., München: Vahlen

Paschke (2001), Grundlagen der Volkswirtschaftslehre anschaulich dargestellt, Heidenau: PD-Verlag.

Pelikan, P. (2004), "Interconnecting Evolutionary, Institutional and Cognitive Economics: Six Steps towards Understanding the Six Links", Contribution to the 10th Meeting of J.A. Schumpeter International Society in Milan, June 9-12, 2004.

Polanyi, K. ([1944] 1997), The Great Transformation. Politische und ökonomische Ursprünge von Gesellschaften und Wirtschaftssystemen. Frankfurt/M.: Suhrkamp.

Ritschard, G. (1983), "Qualitative Comparative Static Techniques", Econometrica, 51 (4), pp. 1145-1168.

Samuelson, P. (1947), Foundations of Economic Analysis. Cambridge Mass.: Harvard University Press.

Sen, A. (1993), "On the Darwinian View of Progress", Population and Development Review, Vol. 19, No. 1, pp. 123-137.

Slutsky, E. ([1915] 1953), On the Theory of the Budget of the Consumer.

Smith, A. ([1776] 1976), An inquiry into the nature and causes of the wealth of nation, Oxford: Clarendon Press.

Tinbergen, J. (1935), "Annual Survey: Suggestions on Quantitative Business Cycle Theory". Econometrica, III, 1935, pp. 241-308.

Walras, L. ([1926] 1954), Elements of Pure Economics or the theory of social wealth. (Translated by William Jaffé from: Walras, L. (1874) Elements d'economie politique pure. Lausanne, Corbaz) Homewood, Ill.: Irwin.

Wildmann, L. (2012), Wirtschaftspolitik. Module der Volkswirtschaftslehre Vol. III, 2nd ed. München: Oldenbourg

Is Competitiveness Development Self-Defeating Through Its Impact on Social Structures and Values?

Jean-Pierre Gern
(Neuchâtel, Switzerland)

1. Introduction

What are we to understand from: competitiveness development in the EU?

Competitiveness is generally considered as the capacity to produce the same good as others at a comparable price. For *Adam Smith* (1776), the (absolute) advantage meant a smaller number of hours of work. For *David Ricardo* (1821) a greater number of hours of work could be compensated by a lower one in other productions: comparative advantage. Today the comparison is made in price and implies the rate of exchange of currencies and transaction costs. If we consider all the transaction costs, which have to be borne by the enterprise directly or indirectly, competitiveness depends on many other factors.

Competitiveness is understood differently at the level of enterprises or at the level of a country or a union, such as the EU:

- For an enterprise it is practically its ability to compete with similar enterprises. The issue of competitiveness for an enterprise is facing competition, and its ability to face competition is measured by its ability to make profits.
- For a country or a union like the EU the relationship to its partners is not considered merely for one product or even for one sector, but for the whole economy; it comes down to its ability to balance its external exchanges, globally or with a specific partner.

2. The actors of competitiveness development and their strategies

The strategies for competitiveness development are consequently different at the different levels:

2.1. Strategy of enterprises

In a world, where markets are very open and competition quite strong, the strategy of enterprises is to impose themselves on the markets and consequently to increase their power: new markets, a higher share of the market, domination of the market. It implies increasing and securing the money value of their sales and minimising their costs. Creating demand and accumulating capital are key factors. Beyond day-to-day competitiveness, enterprises are anxious to secure their share in a "global economy" and consequently loosen their tie with their country of origin.

To increase their competitiveness they have three main lines of action:
- decreasing costs,
- enlarging and dominating the market for their products and
- reinforcing their strategic position.

2.1.1 Decreasing costs

Most often mentioned is the decrease in wages and salaries. The purpose is to bring them more in line with the level of poorer countries, where remuneration and cost of living are low.

Another way of decreasing costs is a shift to more capital intensive methods. In the face of a decrease in demand, the Swiss Post Office moved to automatic sorting ... creating thus a great, possibly critical, rigidity in the cost structure.

Besides, there are two ways of outsourcing: either to poorly paid local companies or to lower income countries. The former reinforces economic and social dualism of the country. The latter is transferring, often unconsciously, industry to the competitors of tomorrow. Typically the pharmaceutical industry is transferring the production of the active elements for drugs to Asia.

A less visible way is shifting costs to others, mainly to the public sector, mainly a pressure on taxes or for subsidies, the additional burden going to taxpayers in general.

The concentration of enterprises in the locations most favourable for themselves, mainly in large cities and on the best communication lines, may decrease their cost, but it increases social expenditures and creates problematic structures for the future.

2.1.2 Enlarging and dominating the markets

As enterprises measure their competitiveness by their capacity to maintain and increase their sales at profitable prices, any action aiming at selling more or at a higher price is a positive factor for their competitiveness.

To increase the value of their sales enterprises continuously invest both human and financial resources in enlarging their market. Especially on the internal market they have many ways of achieving this purpose:
- creating new needs by all possible means (fashion, gadgets, bonuses and lottery attached to any kind of goods or services, technical changes...),
- "opening, or creating the market" by publicity, nowadays 360 degrees publicity,
- purchasing all smaller enterprises in their field, even unprofitable ones, thanks to their financial power,
- obtaining patents not for significant innovations but in order to block the way of competitors,

- conditioning the behaviour of the whole population: even when they seem to answer the expectations of the customers, they may have created the expectations.

Such strategies apply mainly to the European market, where they sell most of their production. For other markets, they are also putting pressure on the political power to ease their exports, for instance with trade agreements, which may be problematic for other local industries (typically for agriculture in Switzerland).

2.1.3. Reinforcing their strategic position

To reinforce their strategic position enterprises aim at a domination of the productive system itself. The present game of the main multinational companies all across the planet is illustrative of such a policy. To secure competitiveness, they aim at controlling their relationships both upstream and downstream (vertical integration) and to develop worldwide their productive capacities in order not only to be present on the market but also to dominate the productive sector. The competition between Nestlé and Unilever, which is spreading all over the world, is characteristic of this.

2.2. Strategy of political powers

Around the world, strategies are quite different, especially between Asian and Western countries. We shall limit ourselves to Europe. Political action in this field looks like a strange mixture of traditional and ideological elements complemented with remedial opportunistic interventions. Traditionally European governments strengthened the competitiveness of their economy by the support they gave to their industries, mainly for export, through various tools, often at the expense of the whole economy. At the macroeconomic level they put pressure on the rate of inflation, the rate of interest or the rate of exchange. They also sign trade agreements with other countries. They try to improve the productive capacity through innovations.

These strategies are generally facing immediate problems. They sometimes consider structural changes in a longer term perspective (e.g. iron and steel in Europe). But they are limited in their view to the direct effect of their action on the competitiveness of the productive system concerned.

3. Competitiveness development versus social values and structures

We call "social structures" the structures of society in all fields, including institutions, norms, organisation of economic and other activities as well as human resources. Values mainly refer to culture ("*Volkskultur*" and "*Kunstkultur*"). Behaviours are involved as they belong to "*Volkskultur*".

If social structures and values have an impact on competitiveness, they are also modified by the strategies aiming at competitiveness development.

The relation between the productive sector and the socioeconomic environment is specific to every sociocultural area. Even if the productive system develops on a worldwide scale, there will always be sociocultural and structural differences between regions.

Therefore the ability of the European economy to compete on the world market may be increased or decreased by the efforts of its enterprises to be more competitive and of the political powers to support them. The effect is, of course, different in the short term and in the long term. Most relevant is the long term competitiveness of the European economy, as it will be more and more challenged by newcomers.

The question we have to face is not just the competitiveness of individual companies, but of a given economic area, like the EU. Increasing the competitiveness of some companies may decrease the global competitiveness and consequently also the competitiveness of those companies. Except for foreign companies settled somewhere in the world without relation to their environment (like mining companies in Third World countries, or trade and banking in city-states), there is a significant relationship between a company and the efficiency of its environment. How do they interact with each other? How do competitiveness development of enterprises and the action of governments to support them, modify their environment? And what backlash effect should be expected?

4. Impact of competitiveness development on social structures and values and backlash consequences

To answer the question of the impact of competitiveness development on social structures and values and of the backlash consequences, we cannot build a general model, as circumstances are complex and the interrelations between factors may vary. The best we can do is to suggest a few examples of such occurrences:

Presently enterprises, even among the most profitable ones, tend to increase their profit in order to strengthen their competitiveness through a significant decrease in employment. This increases unemployment and the weight of social compensations; and with time it may also contribute to the creation of large pockets of population expelled from the productive system. As well, in order to compete with countries, where social conditions are much poorer, companies force down wages or give labour intensive work to poorly paying subcontractors. The loss of purchasing power of an increasing share of the population has a dramatic effect on the dynamics of the internal economy. *John Maynard Keynes* has shown how a society, which does not increase consumption in relation to its national income, ruins its market and degrades its productive capacity. It is first a question of the coherence and of the dynamics of the economic flows. But it is also a question of the impact on socioeconomic structures.

The strength of an economy and of its capacity for development is largely dependent on the density and the quality of its internal flow network. Physiocrates have convincingly shown its significance. The development of economic structures and the profitability of all activities depends on the coherence and the dynamism of the national network of exchanges. European companies produce mainly for the European market; export activities are a stimulus, but also a risk through time. In the long term, the strength and the performance of the economy rest on the coherence of its internal structures.

When enterprises use all possible ways to increase the value of their sales on the internal market, they indirectly increase their costs, as wages and salaries are pushed up by the increase in transaction costs and artificial needs.

As more capitalist production requires higher and more stable sales, publicity developed since the end of the 19th century. Presently it is getting out of proportion, well beyond the cost of production itself in many sectors. What does it mean for an economic area like Europe, when trading and publicity outweigh production in terms of the use of resources (human and financial) and of its share in national product?

Should we understand that, with the same amount of resources Europe could produce far more, up to twice as much? In other words, employment and production structures are biased in a way, which makes it difficult to improve competitiveness, though the resources for such an improvement are there.

The creation of demand by producers and traders also has a significant effect on the consumption pattern; need for objects without real utility has an impact on social culture, which raises questions. The consequent change in socioeconomic structures and culture reduces the capacity of the economy concerned to compete with others. The rational satisfaction of needs in the national economy may have more influence on competitiveness on the world market than the level of wages and salaries. Consequently increasing competitiveness at the European level not only needs improving the productive sector but also developing a new way of social organisation and of living, not more modest but more rational.

When enterprises concentrate their activities in areas where the access to main roads, train and airport is best, mainly in urban areas, the public sector has to finance more and more investments and services. Increasing public investment or public charges for urbanisation, transportation and communication is a long lasting hindrance to competitiveness.

When enterprises transfer costs to other social actors – especially: consumers or political institutions – they cannot escape contributing to the cost borne by others: higher salaries or higher taxes. When they succeed in escaping it, as is the case in the last decade, social and economic dualism rises in the country.

When the aim and tools of competitiveness development concentrates on enterprises active in the world market, the low productivity of enterprises working for the local market creates a burden through a higher cost of living. In this respect, the neglect of agriculture in developing countries is typical.

Another element of the fight for competitiveness is the competition on a market which is not given the attention it deserves: the market for enterprises. If finance plays a great role in competition on the market for goods and services, it may have an even greater role on the market for enterprises. Thanks to their financial power, the larger ones, mainly those with an international status, find it easy to absorb all smaller ones. Among them there are many European enterprises, but also an increasing number of foreign enterprises taking over the European ones. And the difference between both may not be as great as it appears, for in both cases the loss of the companies' control of their shareholders creates the danger, that at a regional, national or European level the leading enterprises loose their ties with their European context. To reinforce their strategic position they may prefer to locate themselves outside. If the industrial fabric is not cared for with an adequate industrial policy, the European economy may lose ground, just as it was the case in Third World countries.

If we consider the relation between production costs and transaction costs, we may wonder whether the development of the tertiary sector well beyond industry and agriculture, instead of a progress, is not partially a burden for those activities and compromises their competitiveness in a way which is almost impossible to eradicate, as it is intricately part of the socioeconomic system.

5. Conclusion: competitiveness development in Europe

It appears that the present habit of enterprises to push up their competitiveness and the present support given them by political powers may contribute to the historical receding of the European economy in the global worldwide development. Not only will newcomers gain in importance quantitatively, but also in efficiency relatively to Europe. But it may not be unavoidable. Improved policies may have a positive impact on the relative competitiveness of Europe.

Public policies may prove deceitful, if they are not a part of an economic strategy, which covers all the fields, we have mentioned in the transformation and development of economic and social structures. Some fields may appear to escape governments' policies, for instance the change in behaviours and culture. Who then can be the actors of an efficient increase of competitiveness in the EU?

As the increase in competitiveness does not depend only on the capacity of exporting enterprises, but on the whole socioeconomic system, improving it involves far more decision makers than presently assumed. And it needs a good coordination system within the framework of a well defined strategy. Beyond the fascinating opposition of liberalism against state socialism, an efficient and coherent decision making system has to be elaborated in order to secure a rational change in socioeconomic structures. Many coordinated changes have to be undertaken in all fields to secure the competitiveness of Europe in tomorrow's world economy.

References

Keynes, John Maynard 1936: The General Theory of Employment, Interest and Money, London

Ricardo, David 1821: On the Principles of Political Economy and Taxation, 3rd ed. London

Smith, Adam 1776: An inquiry into the nature and causes of the wealth of nations, London

CHAPTER TWO:

STUDIES ON EUROPEAN ECONOMIES AND POLICY AREAS

BEYOND STATE AND MARKET: TOWARDS A PARTICIPATED GOVERNANCE OF LOCAL PUBLIC UTILITIES?

LUCA BARTOCCI / FRANCESCA PICCIAIA
(UNIVERSITY OF PERUGIA, ITALY)

1. Introduction

The search for a new way of organizing the public sector is a significant problem for many countries, especially in light of the current crisis, which poses the need to provide satisfactory levels of public services in compliance with a condition of financial sustainability.

This need for renewal must be inserted in a stage in which the transition to a new model of public administration had already begun at least in the theoretical debate: the long period inspired by New Public Management (NPM) seems to be at an end, that is why conceptual models are now focusing on the need to establish a new relationship with civil society and citizens, no longer considered as mere customers. Many "labels" are used today (Public Governance, Collaborative Governance, Community Governance, New Public Service, Public Value Management, just to name the most common). They all focus on the search for a new narrative of the relationship between "public" and "private". Supposing that it is actually possible to talk of a new post-managerial era, the need of the civil society for an accountable public administration and the need of citizens to play a central role are still meaningful in the heritage of the NPM.

This is the context where the two central ideas of this work developed: the recovery of an "old" concept of democratic systems, that is participation, and the proposal of another approach, linked to participation and often superficially estimated, the principle of subsidiarity. Our hypothesis is that these "values" can be taken as the cornerstones of a new welfare model, which we define as "subsidiary".

From this theory our research focuses on one particular form of "subsidiarisation" of public action: the involvement of nonprofit organizations (NPOs) in public services management. It is a "third way" between state and market, a way that, besides being of great theoretical suggestion, heavily relies on international experiences discussed hereby. The use of specific forms of NPOs could provide adequate mechanisms for the participation of citizens with significant consequences in terms of accountability.

2. The public sector between old and new conceptual references

In recent decades the public sector has been undergone a profound renewal in all so-called western countries, but probably this has affected
the majority of nations, even those with a lower level of development,
especially because of the dynamic role played by international institutions (M.S. Haque 2000: 599-600). Apparently this happened – and it is
still happening – with varying intensity and with characteristics related
to specific situations, but in international literature many interpretations
are proposed which allow to recognize the rationale behind the different
experiences.

   The starting point is usually located in the transition from the old bureaucratic administration to the spread of the managerialism wave
which has invaded the public agencies worldwide. Starting in the 1980s,
a kind of cultural movement known as New Public Management (NPM)
began to take shape and has promoted an international plan to reform
the public sector (C. Hood 1991: 3-4). There is an almost endless literature on the subject, whose analysis shows that the NPM, rather than being a true paradigm, should be regarded as a sort of umbrella-term, that
gathers a great variety of meanings and contents, able to inspire the main
renewal attempts of the recent decades (C. Hood 1995: 93-109). In this
reflection, some "mega-trends" that underlie the specific cultural model
of the NPM were identified (J. O'Flynn 2007: 354). The first key concept
which needs to be considered is the conviction of the need for downsiz-
ing the public sector and the presence of the State in economy; this
brought to a policy of decentralization and fragmentation of the public
sector. The second key concept is the absolute value of individual freedom and the idea of market as a field of encounter and combination of
individual preferences, with a massive use of privatization or quasi-
privatization techniques and the use of contracting as a privileged rela-
tionship-regulation tool. Linked to this aspect is the assumption of the
centrality of services provision in the relationship between public sector
and citizens, with a compression of the typical government activities (G.
Stoker 2006: 46). Finally, the development of public management is
worth mentioning, seen as a primary actor capable of synthesizing the
moment of political decision and that of technical implementation, being
able to use a rich theoretical and practical framework developed in private law. In the last decade, in the international literature, a deep critical
reflection on the NPM has been undertaken, highlighting its theoretical
limits and applications. The OECD, which has long been one of the institutions mostly engaged in the dissemination of NPM, inspired principles
and practices, admitted that the ongoing reforms have produced unex-
pected negative results (OECD 2003: 2).

First, criticisms are based on the idea that logic and mechanics of market instruments cannot be automatically applied to the public sector and on the differences between public and private management (W. Kickert 1997: 734). More specifically: excessive costs due to the creation of insufficiently competitive markets were highlighted, with particular reference to transaction costs of contracting mechanisms (T. Entwistle/S. Martin 2005: 235-237); the efficiency of applications to solve the loss of accountability has been questioned (Minogue, 2000); according to some, the fragmentation of the sector and the rising competition would produce a negative effect on the "public ethos" (M. Brereton/M. Temple 1999: 458-462), also caused by the risk of exacerbation of the conflict between individual and public interest. Many authors believe that the NPM has had the effect of eroding the traditional social values which make the public action natural (especially legitimacy, representativeness, participation, equity), disaggregating the boundaries of the public sector and making them indefinite, increasing opacity in the function of accountability and liability of the public (L.D. Terry, 1998: 194-200).

A conceptual framework that in recent years has been more and more insistently recalled in this regard is Public Governance (PG). It represents a theoretical approach that relies on the contribution of different disciplines and, for this reason, cannot easily be summarized in a concise and unambiguous definition. In a sense, rather than a punctually structured model, one can speak of a "basic vision" of how to govern the public system (J. Kooiman 1999: 67-92).

Now there is a wide range of doctrinal contributions concerning the issue and significant documents have been published by major international institutions: the World Bank, UNDP, the UN agency, the OECD and the European Union (D. Cepiku 2006: 37-53). This new concept is frequently opposed to the traditional concept of government, which is to say the exercise of decision making resulting from the formal institutional system (E. Borgonovi 2002: 40).

In summary, compared to the "bureaucratic model", governance qualifies for:

- the emergence of a new role of public administration, increasingly oriented to promotion, to "enabling" and to coordination, facilitating the spread of the concept of networks and of partnership concerning both inter-institutional relations and relations between public and private sector;
- increased sensitivity to the political-strategic profiles of the decision-making processes and the search for their integration with bureaucratic systems;

- the inclusion of a large number of actors through the use of consultation and voluntary participation;
- the use of both formal and informal tools in the quest for internal and external consensus;
- attention towards the impact of policies and processes in terms of outcome towards citizens.

The new paradigm shifts the focus from a microeconomic and business-oriented point of view to a more extensive system. Typical aspects of the policy-making process are herewith enhanced, scaling down the possible distortions of management techniques. Another point of view considers the issue of governance a continental alternative to Anglo-Saxon neo-managerialism (W. Kickert 1997: 749-750).

Many authors consider the concept of PG, whatever it is called, a possibility for overcoming the presumed depletion of social values caused by the NPM, recovering the bi-directionality of the relationship between PA and citizens, not considered as customers but as partners (E. Vigoda 2002: 529-530). The model is based on a collaborative logic, with the assistance of a number of subjects aimed at satisfying public needs. Even in terms of accountability, shifting the focus from output to outcome should result in a greater attention to the actual condition of the recipients of public policies, by providing ways to involve them in decisions and evaluations. In this sense, some speak of democratic accountability, stressing the importance of not only the results, but also of the way these results are pursued and implemented.

This new resulting reality is made of a plurality of actors (public and otherwise), linked by a network of relationships governed by a variety of tools (formalized or not). The key reference is not the citizen as such, but as belonging to a community with which it shares a heritage of ideals. The public value to be created can therefore not only be measured by indicators of efficiency and effectiveness, but must be viewed in a more social perspective. It is in this sense that expressions such as collaborative governance, network or community are used (A. Sancino 2010: 117-118).

Maintaining this background vision, we find readings which vary according to the specific underlining of some of the proposed elements. Two of these theoretical elaborations, which have found an independent position in literature, deserve special mention also because they originated within the American environment.

With particular reference to the subject of public service provision, Robert Denhart and Janet Vinzant Denhart have proposed an interesting approach that would overcome the limits of NPM, conveying a different conception of the role of public administration (2000: 549-559). The authors offer their seven-points setting, after indicating as cultural roots of the New Public Service (NPS) – that is how they name their contribution – the political and social theories on democratic citizenship, the studies on models of community and civil society, the approaches on organizational humanism and the Discourse Theory (2000: 553-557). The idea behind this is that the fundamental role of public servants is to help citizens express and meet their shared interests, rather than to act as a control or to push society towards new directions (as symbolically indicated by the phrase "serve rather than steer" as opposed to another phrase "steer rather than row", considered as the synthesis of NPM).

Beyond the criticisms that can be moved to the NPS, it is interesting to remark the spread of attempts to stimulate a new "civic renaissance" in the United States, which rediscovers the concept of community and establishes new relationships between public organizations and civil society (R. Putnam 2005: 7-10).

More concentrated on the production of public value and on the role of management, Mark Moore has published his book *"Creating Public Value: Strategic Management in Government"* (1995), considered as the cornerstone of a new conceptual approach, used by a part of the doctrine in an attempt to strengthen the theoretical foundations of a new era of reform (R.F.I. Smith 2004: 78-79; G. Stoker 2006: 46-49).

Moore begins with the assumption that the creation of public value constitutes the fundamental activity of public managers, as well as the maximization of value for the shareholder is the fundamental purpose of private sector managers. In this sense the task of public management is not only to oversee the processes of the market, but also to balance technical and political issues. In this model a central role is played by the formation of collective preferences which are no longer conceived as the sum of individual preferences, but as formed through mechanisms of participated deliberation (Horney-Hazel 2005: 34; G. Stoker 2006: 42). In the generation of value the production of community services is very important, as well as the normative regulation and the typical activities of government (G. Kelly/G. Mulgan/S. Muers 2000: 4-9). In other words, the Public Value (PV) would qualify as an alternative to the NPM framework, based on a more pragmatic approach that goes beyond an uncritical confidence in the market (G. Stoker 2006: 47-49). The pragmatism of the PV has been proposed as a way to overcome a vision based on the research for the one best way that has characterized the last decades (J. Alford/O. Hughes 2008: 138-140).

Again, also in this case there are critical positions, mostly related to the incompleteness of its theoretical foundations; in particular, the vagueness of the concept of public value (J. Benington 2009: 233) and the persistence of the reference to the private sector, especially in the excessively central role attributed to management (R. Rhodes/J. Wanna 2007: 409-411).

From this picture we highlight that the present moment is marked by a variety of positions which, though agreeing with the theory of overcoming the NPM, promote different points of view. This is a phase of development which is not yet completed, in which approaches appear to be less anchored to monolithic and closed visions. This is also confirmed by the observation of practice; the use of tools and techniques of NPM cannot be considered as totally overcome and in certain cases there is also a return to more traditional approaches (R.F.I. Smith 2004: 74). This is not unrelated to the effects of the ongoing financial and economic crisis, which produced a tendency to reaffirm the centrality of the State (A. Sancino 2010: 117). There are also those who, with reference to the countries of continental Europe, envisage the formation of a Neo-Weberian model, characterized by the spread of hybrid organizations that blend rules of the "old" bureaucracy with more innovative values and techniques (S. Kuhlmann 2010: 1128). In any case, it seems undeniable that in the background two essential principles stand out that no attempt at renewal can escape: the opening of public systems to the logics of competition and the search for instruments of greater democratization (B.G. Peters 2008: 195).

3. Participation and subsidiarity as conditions for good governance

We have seen how the growing interest for governance is caused by the necessity to assign renewed meanings and values to political action, in order to guarantee the quality of that system of relations which has deteriorated over time. Many authors stressed the fact that the opening out of public systems can only take place in an adequate way if the civil society is involved (Q. Bruguè/R. Gallego 2003: 425-447; L. Bingham/T. Nabatchi/R. O'Leary 2005: 547-558). All these factors are speeding up the public world towards the testing of new forms of cooperation representing an alternative to the hierarchical as well as to the pure-market models of governance (R. Rhodes 1996: 652-667; R. Mayntz 1999: 3-22).

The problem is also influenced by two connected renewal tendencies, very well known in Italy as well. On the one hand we find the research for new methods and tools which increase the influence of civil society in the decision-making processes of governance and which consider the participation of citizens to public policies. On the other, there is the attention to the system conditions through the pursuit of innovative structures and policies aiming at creating virtuous mechanisms of confrontation, subrogation and collaboration between the State and other subjects operating in the system (public utilities, companies, nonprofit organizations, families etc.), by stressing the importance of subsidiarity.

The subject of participation in public governance systems dates back to the 1950s and 60s, but has been particularly investigated during the last decade. Many works underlined its meanings (R. Kluvers/S. Pillay 2009: 220-230), goals (S. Royo/A. Yetano/B. Acerete 2011: 139-150), levels and tools (A. L. Franklin/A. T. Ho/C. Ebdon 2009: 52-73), the premises for success (Cuthill-Fien 2005: 63-80), and the limits of applicability (K. Callahan 2007: 1179-1196). To make a synthesis, it is possible to distinguish three different cultural stances which underlie the application of participative practices:

(1) the achievement of new approaches aiming at recovering the concept of democracy in those contexts where the inefficacy of systems founded on representative mechanisms is denounced (K. Callahan 2007:1179-1196);

(2) the recognition of the necessity to recover legitimation and trust in public action, in a perspective of social cohesion empowerment and community construction (M. Cuthill/J. Fien 2005: 63-80; A. Novy/ B. Leubolt 2005: 2023-2036);

(3) the focalization, mainly in the Anglo-Saxon world, on the benefits in terms of performance improvement and public organizations accountability (R. Kluvers/S. Pillay 2009: 220-230; C. Skelcher/J. Torfing 2010: 71-91).

The opportunity to promote participative practices has been the main subject developed by international organizations. The main concept is the achievement of a new idea of citizens who should be seen as a co-actor of the governance action (P. Bishop/G. Davis 2002: 14-15).

The first significant contribution in this field is represented by the OECD document entitled *"Citizens as Partners: Information, Consultation and Public Participation in Policy Making"* (OECD 2001).

This paper provides elements aiming at improving the relationship between institutions and citizens, given as one of the main characteristics of good governance. In this perspective, the paper stresses the necessity of democratic governments to strengthen the participation of citizens in order to improve the quality of policies, responding to the growing request for accountability, and reinforcing trust in the administration.

In the document three different levels of involvement are distinguished:

• *information*, meant as a one-way relationship in which government authorities produce and release information for citizens;

- *consultation*, meant as a two-way relationship in which citizens give a feedback to government authorities through appropriate procedures;
- *active participation*, meant as a relationship based on collaboration, in which citizens actively take part in the decision making processes, although the responsibility for the final choice and the resulting policies remains in the hands of governmental authorities.

Another important reference is given by the documents produced by the World Bank in which a new concept of accountability is proposed, making reference to the concepts of governance, effectiveness of development politics and empowerment. The idea is that a government, apart from reporting on its institutional role in terms of respect of the law and of efficient, effective, and fair management of resources (government accountability), has also a social accountability, that is its interpretation of the relationship with the civil society, since nowadays the involvement of citizens is recognized as a fundamental element for the improvement of its work (World Bank 1997 and 2004).

Also the works published by the United Nations and in particular by the UNDP deal with the issue of civil society involvement as a factor of development and of a democratic governance. More in detail, participatory practices are seen as a qualifying factor for local governments. The main points of a study on the role of participation and partnership in decentralized governance underline the importance of:

- the importance of the contribution of the civil society, also in view of the reduction of the negative effects of administrative and professional technicalities;
- the importance of civil participation in the legitimating process of local authorities and the promotion of trust and of the cooperation culture;
- the facilitation of the community involvement in public decision processes and in decentralized governance;
- the efficiency of participation mechanisms when they are institutionalized.

The importance of citizens participation to public decision processes was reaffirmed in 2007 by the UN in the Vienna Declaration called *"Building Trust in Government"*, where the subject was inserted in the good governance set of rules.

From the community point of view, the European Council issued a recommendation on the participation of citizens in public life, where the Member States are invited to subscribe to the general principles and to pledge to improve inclusive practices.

In general, it is possible to state that in institutional documents the promotion of active participation is proposed through two main ways: the direct initiative of citizens through established legal institutions and the possibility for putting in practice political "open" decision processes even using less formal tools. This second option is particularly appreciated in that group of studies on political and legal sciences, where the theory of "deliberative democracy" is promoted. This concept is based on a new idea of deliberation extended to the whole process of decision making and not only to the final part. In this case political power is not anymore the only centre of political decision and the task of government institutions becomes that of encouraging social-political interactions aiming at solving problems (J. Elster 1998).

The issue of citizens inclusion into governance mechanisms shows some points of contact and analogy with a principle which has been recognized in some official documents published by supranational institutions, particularly in Europe, but which at the same time is almost absent in the international doctrinal reflection: the principle of subsidiarity.

It is known that the first complete enunciation of this principle has been given by Pope Pius XI. In his encyclical *"Quadragesimo anno"* promulgated in 1931, he declared that

"as it is gravely wrong to take from individuals what they can accomplish by their own initiative and industry and give it to the community, so also it is an injustice and at the same time a grave evil and disturbance of right order to assign to a greater and higher association what lesser and subordinate organizations can do."

The document thus proposes an approach which goes beyond the religious boundaries and establishes a hierarchy in the initiative power of the different subjects operating in a socio-economic system, stating that the aim of every action in society is *"to furnish help to the members of the social body, and never destroy and absorb them"*.

This reference has evident consequences for the cultural, political, economical, and social point of view, as it gives a vision of the State and of the relationship between the public system and the civil community based on the centrality of man and of his associative expressions (G. Vittadini, 2007: 17-26). Moreover, this concept represents the formalization of an idea of society based on the active role of intermediate bodies which belongs to the European historical and cultural tradition since the Middle-Ages (E. Bressan 2007: 101-112).

It is our opinion that this paradigm, as it is intrinsic to the very notion of State and of its relation with the subjects constituting its reference community, represents an important base for the creation of a new public governance. More precisely, from a political and cultural point of view, this can constitute the foundation of institutional structures and governances aiming at enhancing the citizens' freedom of choice and the demand for leadership expressed by an increasing part of the civil society, thus stimulating the concretization of the principle which recognizes that public action has to work for the common good (S. Zamagni 1998: 46).

This corresponds to the role of "qualifier" and "regulator" that the paradigm of PG gives to the public sector and, at the same time, encourages the recovery of a positive dialectic between the public sector itself and citizens. This recovery can overcome the legitimacy and consensus crisis afflicting our institutions.

The approach can have important consequences also in terms of growth of the effectiveness and efficiency of public action. The search for a synergetic relation with the civil society allows for a better interpretation of the community needs and the definition of new intervention methods responding to those needs.

All these elements foreshadow the possibility for coming to a new image of the society where the different public and private operators compete in providing public services. This would mean to realize the passage from the traditional welfare state to a subsidiary state (also defined as welfare society and welfare mix), characterized by the presence of a plurality of subjects whose aim is, apart from their juridical nature, to try and give answers to the social need expressed by community (L. Fazzi 2000; J. Rodger 2000).

4. Collaboration relations between "public" and "private" in the management of public services

According to the framework provided, we can distinguish three levels of reasons that still give a central role to the possibility of interaction between the public and private sector.

First of all, it has to be noted that the presumed overcoming of NPM does not exclude the possibility of delegating productive and distribution functions of public services. Instead, the uncritical trust towards competition is challenged; the necessity to verify the applicability of market logics is quoted; more collaborative approaches which consider the citizen not just as client are recommended. At the same time the pressing necessity for a coordination role of the public activity is notified, as it would be useful to promote an organized action in a system composed of numerous public and non public actors (W. Kickert 1997: 731-752). It is necessary to specify that there are also perspectives which tend to enhance the continuity between NPM and the newest paradigms. The latter can be interpreted as an evolution of NPM, without emphasizing the differences between the two (R. Mussari 1998: 181; M. Mene-guzzo 1997: 592-593; D. Cepiku 2005: 119-121).

The second level is represented by the fact that the approach which is more and more spreading nowadays lost some of its previous ideological connotation and by the idea that a better public performance can be reached through different solutions. The pragmatism of the PV model makes the possible solutions relative while giving more attention to specific local situations. The use of contracting, the strong point of NPM in the management of public services, is contested but not denied: it must be evaluated according to its practicality and to the production of social value (J. Alford/O. Hughes 2008: 140-143).

The last level concerns the importance of the development of subsidiarity, as a principle which can propose a different and deeper interpretation of the action of stakeholders and of the role of the public sector. This vision appeals to the constructive and socializing desire of mankind, a sort of "positive anthropology" at the base of sociality, and considers the associative reality the most adequate to guarantee room for actual freedom and activity of mankind (A. Brugnoli/G. Vittadini (eds.) 2008: 20-25). From this point of view, non-profit organizations have a great potential as their goal is genetically focused on the satisfaction of social needs without the primacy of profit.

Literature and practice give us a wide variety of institutional solutions with different suggestions for the interaction between public institutions and individuals in the supply of services to the community. If we exclude the cases of complete privatization, it is possible to distinguish the following categories of technical solutions (V.R. Johnston/P. Seidenstat 2007: 233-236):

- *Partnerships.* There can be different forms of cooperation between private and public sectors, through which competences and resources are combined in order to realize and manage infrastructure works according to the many responsibilities and goals possible. In public-private partnership projects, PA usually entrusts the private operator with the realization and management of public works or utilities. In Italy the most common form is the so-called "project financing", but there are also other forms concerning social services and not infrastructures.
- *Contracting.* It represents the entrusting of public services management to external private subjects (contracting out) or public subjects (contracting in), regulated by a concession contract. Usually the property of the structures necessary to the production/supply of the service remains public. There is a rare variety of contracting, in which the private subject is the provider of services technically pro-

duced by public operators. Competitive contracting is another possibility: competition mechanisms are created among different public
and private subjects, also dividing the service into different parts.
• *Quasi-markets*. They are designed to create mechanisms of choice for
citizens who are in front of a variety of offers from private and public operators, for example through vouchers or subsidies. The word
"quasi" (literally *"almost"*) defines the particular conditions to
which both demand and supply are subjected: the former offers a
price using funds which are at least in part public; the latter is constituted of a plurality of subjects exposed to accreditation procedures and which are in the last resort financed by the public sector.
The public sector plays a role of promotion and regulation of the
system (J. Le Grand 1990: 1256-1267);
• *Voluntary activity*. It is the case of services voluntary offered to a
public organization by citizens or non-profit organizations. The intervention of the private can consist in forms of collaboration or the
complete outsourcing of the activities conducted under the super-
vision or the coordination of the public administration.
It has to be noted that in all of these cases, even if at different degrees,
what is stressed is the separation between the political responsibility of
the public institution and the management responsibility of the subject
which has been entrusted to guarantee the technical production and the
distribution of the service. This dichotomy is based on the distinction between two concepts: function and service. The former defines the institutional responsibility in a given social area, politically recognized, where a
social need is expressed; the latter defines the technical activity aiming at
satisfying this need. The previously recalled public sector reform trends
emphasized the guidance, control and guarantee of public operators, re-
lieving the productive organizations from many of their characteristic
tasks and/or transforming their role of majority shareholders of the fi-
duciary societies into that of system regulators.

5. The possible way of "non profit"

The overcoming of the direct intervention (*govern*) as a privileged way of
providing public services should allow for opening this sector to a possible competitive market, in which the mechanism of the automatic protection of the monopolist (*incumbent*) fails and in which, in case of outsourcing, the service contract becomes particularly prominent, as it defines the
relationship between the two parties and the provision's conditions (M.
Elefanti 2003a: 150-175; C. San Mauro 2004: 23-58). This situation clearly
introduces some problems concerning the governance of these utilities

and of the accountability of the operators involved in this system (M. Elefanti 2003b: 27-35).

A first aspect regards the quality of the relationship between the regulator and the provider of the public services. Some scholars – especially in the UK where there has been an ongoing privatisation process of public services for decades – have highlighted an adversarial relationship between providers and regulators (G. Holtham 1997: 3-8). This critical aspect could make some theoretically successful processes ineffective (N. Prasad 2006: 669-692). The reasons of this conflict would be found in two basic weaknesses, not concerning the failure of the functions of the regulator *per se*, but the wrong belief that a simple change of the ownership and of the service management is sufficient to guarantee a competitive process (J. Kay 1996: 28-46). The first fundamental limit is that the privatisation process would lack of legitimacy («*what gives them the right to do that?*»). Whereas this aspect is rarely a problem when the government directly manages the public services, because it acts as provided by the electoral mandate, in case of a private party, although chosen through a public competition, this could become a critical element.

Secondly, there is the risk of not increasing the efficiency of the provision in terms of costs that causes the informative asymmetry between the government-regulator and the private-provider. The latter, indeed, has an advantage in terms of price-fixing and consequently it also offers the possibility for carrying out an opportunistic behaviour (J. Kay 1996: 28-46). The final result is an erosion of public value (H. De Brujin/W. Dicke 2006: 717-735) and a consequent unpopularity of the system that does not permit to underline sufficiently the advantages of the privatisation process (increasing efficiency, agencies' simplification, services enhancement, fast response to changes) (R. Miranda/M. Lerner 1995: 193-200; W. Megginson/J. Netter 2001: 321-389).

The problems of the regulator, in the field of controls and of relationship between the "actors" of the system, increase the importance of the institutional and organisational peculiarities of the producer/provider. So, it is fundamental to choose the right institutional form, because the institutional mechanisms are a kind of regulation of behaviours, through incentives and sanctions. In any case, in order to overcome the problem of lacking legitimacy of private organisations, hence to safeguard the correct functioning of the process, a lot of studies point out that the necessary basis to start from has to be shifted from stockholders' safeguard to users' safeguard (H. Hansmann 1996: 163-207; L.B. Morse 2000: 467-495).

Starting from these elements, some surveys have pointed out the possibility for identifying some criteria in order to pick out the best provider's institutional and organisational structure. In particular, according to Birchall (2002: 181-213), the optimal interlocutor of the government should:

- *safeguard the interests of users*. In a natural monopoly, like that of the vast majority of utilities, the conventional ways of organizing a company cannot make it sure for citizens to have an appropriate *voice*. The lack of a plurality of suppliers weakens the citizens and introduces contractual failures and the satisfaction of shareholders' interests can carry out to the detriment of consumers. In this perspective, when choosing a more adequate structure, it is necessary to consider the form that allows the participation to the decisions also to those who are not owners but only recipients of the supply;
- *transcend the limit of a heavy regulation regime*. In those countries where privatisation has already been introduced, the providers' control mechanisms and the management of conflicts between different parties are often far too complex and costly. In this sense, the choice should be that of structures which can reduce and settle differences in the stakeholders' differences, by harmonizing their preferences towards a shared purpose. So, the control structure becomes less heavy and rigid and then less costly and more flexible;
- *incentivize increasing management efficiency*. In all companies it is necessary to deeply examine the problem of how to ensure efficiency and effectiveness of management with adequate incentives. The difficulty in the public utilities' sector is to avoid the alignment between management and ownership goals (so called "producer capture") to the detriment of the consumers. Thus, there are problems concerning the research of alternative incentives for management in order to allow an overlap with those of the consumers;
- *raise capital relatively cheaply*. The management of a natural monopoly should be a low-risk activity and this should consequently decrease the financial costs. In the privatisation process of public utilities, it is necessary that, even when raising capital, companies have the possibility to do that at cheaper conditions. Generally, however, these are sectors that represent low-risk investments for the investors, so profit rates are quite moderate (D. Thomas 2001: 99-114).

On this basis, the author suggests that the NPO is the institutional structure which is potentially more adequate in order to perform production and provision of public utilities.

These are, indeed, organisational forms without a direct financial stake of specific individuals (J. Bennett/E. Iossa/G. Legrenzi 2003: 335-347) and this characteristic allows for narrowing the possibility of abuses of some categories of stakeholders on others. This element is also enforced by the "non-distribution constraint" that solves the problem of a natural monopoly, removing the profit maximisation for investors. Besides, in the NPO's reality there is a strong influence between ideal motivations and business elements (E. Borgonovi 1996: 273). For this reason, NPOs are privileged places of stakeholders' participation in the provision process. This situation enables to maintain all conflicts among stakeholders within the organisation and so to concur to their resolution with a direct interaction between individuals. In this way, every customer participates in providing the utility with positive effects in terms of legitimating of processes and of accountability (S. Sacchetti/E. Tortia 2008: 104-124).

6. The participated governance of NPOs

These latter remarks allow us to introduce a further conceptual step: the importance of participation models within governance, especially regarding non-profit institutions.

In the wider debate about corporate governance and corporate social responsibility, a branch of studies emerges. It is focused on the meanings and the effects of the stakeholders' participation within business organisations. This is called *Multistakeholder Governance* (MSHG) and it identifies a set of organisational practices which can involve individuals, who *ex lege* do not have formal control rights on the assignment of profits (D. Dragone/M. Viviani 2007: 11). Starting from the assumption that there are rules that assign to some individuals formal and substantial control rights on the company's structure, the MSHG is a management model that focuses on the involvement of stakeholders, including those who are formally excluded from the control power they have.

This organisational structure has been more deeply analysed in the field of organisations providing so-called social goods, namely those public goods whose use is non-rivalrous and non-exclusionary. These goods have recently benefited from a process aimed at widening the supply by non-governmental organisations (P. Donati 2004: 23-42; L. Sacconi 2005: 133-156; M. Viviani 2006: 120-145; L. Fazzi 2008: 193-225).

Though having extremely different ways of stakeholders' participation that makes it very difficult to "categorize" actual experiences, a lot of surveys highlight the advantages of the implementation of participation models within non-profit organisations, especially those structuring their activities with entrepreneurship forms. In particular, we can deal with general advantages and specific advantages.

General advantages concern the kind of performed activity: NPOs, indeed, provide a particular product that has the characteristics of social goods. This special output is produced and provided through a "personalized" process, which is structured on the needs of the customer who shares, somehow, the supply of the same product. The primary role of the customer in the goods distribution process goes hand in hand with the essential and basic presence of the operators within the NPOs and the public institutions that sustain these organisations. Therefore, starting from this structure, the implementation of those governance's models, that envisage the involvement of internal and external individuals, allows for the structuring and the improvement of a sharing project that is substantially already present, making the services provision process easier.

Concerning special advantages, these elements comply with different aspects, all of these however refer to an improvement of performances. Firstly, the implementation of participation models permits a reduction of the most common risks in NPOs. A lot of scholars now assert that the non-distribution constraint is inadequate to eliminate the risks of self-reliance and opportunism that could result from the presence of asymmetric information between the organisation and the customers and, more generally, by the incompleteness of contracts (D.R. Young 2001: 139-157; U. Ascoli 2003: 295-310; C. Borzaga 2003: 14-28; L. Fazzi, 2007: 35-50; G. Maino 2008: 125-162).

So, the presence of forms which involve the recipients of the activities facilitates the diffusion (and the reliability) of information and reduces the risk that only one group of stakeholders monopolizes information. Furthermore the sharing of the decisional and organisational power would allow implementing cross controls on performed actions. This is indeed a very important element for some kind of social goods, because of the difficulty to introduce traditional analysis systems (L. Sacconi/M. Faillo 2005: 82-96).

Another element related to the advantages of participated governance concerns the improvement of the qualitative level of the obtained output (L. Fazzi 2007: 63-97; S. Depedri 2008a: 34-54; S. Sacchetti/E. Tortia 2008: 104-124) derived from mutual trust and collaboration between the different groups of individuals. In fact where MSHG is introduced, the large number of "relational" combinations permits to widen the interpretative plans and represents a way to increase the problems' solutions (more inclined to problem solving). The better circulation of information, through the presence of the so-called social capital, indeed, also sustains the production of technical and organisational "productive knowledge" that positively affects the quality of the outputs and, consequently, the level of the obtained social value. Furthermore, it is necessary to consider the strong rooting in the territory of NPOs, that derive human and financial resources from the local context where they provide their services (S. Depedri 2008b: 72-103). Inclusive practices involving local actors allow for the development of these resources and have positive effects in terms of a better compliance between the output and the demand for social goods by the referred environment.

Clearly, the implementation of GMSH models increases the managerial and administrative complexity (derived from both the necessity of harmonising the physiological differences of participants in terms of needs and expectations and the difficulty to coordinate them operationally) and costs (related to a system which is more and more bureaucratic). For this reason, it is fundamental to search for tools that facilitate their sustainability. Many studies highlight that the main tools to safeguard the functioning of shared organisations are related to the strengthening of managerial and control tools that permit to manage the business complexity as good as possible (L. Fazzi 2008: 193-225; M. Franch/E. Leonardi 2008: 226-238) and of the informative and communicative flow that has to unify the different groups of stakeholders in order to stimulate participation (F. Fortuna 2001: 45-47; T.W. Hartley 2006: 115-126). Furthermore, some scholars highlight the basic role of a "cultural share" among participants and of a convergence on the organisation's goals, that could decrease coordination costs, even if this could cause an "over-equalisation" and a consequent limitation of the capacity to face environmental variance (D. Dragone/M. Viviani 2007: 163-192).

7. Some international experiences

In the previous paragraphs we dealt with the possibility of sustaining the privatisation process within the public utilities' sector through NPOs. This idea is also supported by some scholars and it is based on some international experiences. These are examples in which the implementation of inclusive models takes place in different ways. Hence, some cases are highlighted, pointing out briefly the more relevant elements.

Glas Cymru (www.glascymru.com) is a company created by a private initiative in 2000 in order to acquire the assets of Dwr Cymru, an organisation for the provision of Welsh water.

The acquisition (the previous owner was American Western Power Distribution) was completed in 2001 and since then Glas Cymru has the responsibility to supply drinking water and to treat and properly dispose of wastewater all over the region and in some neighbouring areas. It is a company limited by guarantee, a private initiative NPO. As far as the financing is concerned, Glas uses bonds which are traded on the capital market and assessed by business analysts. Every positive economic result is used for a discount in the bills of the customers. Regarding the organisational structure, Glas Cymru is composed of 81 members, 11 of them sit in the *Board of Directors* (1 chairman, 3 executive directors and 7 non executive directors) and are responsible for the strategic direction of the company and for reviewing operational and financial performances. An independent panel (*Membership Selection Panel*) supervises the selection of the members through an open process of nomination. The panel "ensures that the company has a balanced and diverse membership which is as broad as possible and which reflects the interests of customers and other stakeholders served by Welsh Water" (Glas Cymru, 2009: 18). The application is personal that is why the member does not represent any lobby within the company, does not receive any fee and does not have any financial interest in Glas. Communication with other stakeholders is guaranteed through an annual membership meeting, during which it is possible for all participants to meet personally. For stockholders, instead, an annual meeting about periodical results is organized in London.

Nav Canada (www.navcanada.ca) is a "non-share capital private corporation", a private NPO that was created in 1996 by the combined initiative of the Canadian government and some airlines and unions. Their belief was that a private organisation could manage the civil transportation services better than a state-owned one. Now, the company owns and operates Canada's civil *Air Navigation Service* (ANS). *Nav Canada* is financed by the publicly-traded debt. Its organizational structure reflects the coexistence of both public and private stakeholders. *Nav Canada* is particularly focused on safeguarding expectations of every stakeholder in the aviation sector. The company is managed by a Board of 15 members, 5 of whom are appointed by airlines, 3 by the Canadian government, 2 by unions and 4 are independent. Among them a chief executive is chosen with an operational and representative role. There is an advisory committee as well, in which members are appointed at every annual company's meeting in order to relate to stakeholders. Its members are aviation professionals, distinguished in their individual areas of expertise, representing a broad cross-section of Canada's aviation community. "They include professional pilots, air traffic controllers, flight service specialists, technicians, airport and air service operators, and officers of international, national and regional aviation organizations" (www.navcanada.ca).

In the United States the phenomenon of participated governance in the public utilities' sector is locally very widespread, so that it represents an interesting place of experiences of functional dialog between the public and the private. One of the most frequent forms is governance through municipal utilities, a public foundation similar to an NPO (P. Garrone 2010: 130). Management and administration of these organisations are delegated to citizens who live in the provided areas and they privilege the needs of the customers they represent.

One relevant example is the *Detroit Water and Sewerage Department* (www.dwsd.org) that operates in the water sector. From the organisational point of view, there is the *Board of Water Commissioners*, composed of 7 members appointed by the mayor and chosen among all residents in the city and in neighbouring counties. Also in this case, all profits are reinvested and the City of Detroit does not receive any payment or any fee.

Another typology, mainly diffused in rural or decentralised areas, is the utility cooperative. It is an institution created after the New Deal in order to diffuse electric and telephone services in rural regions, not provided by national companies. These organisations are owned and managed by every customer who is also a resident in that area. They all have the same decision power, in respect to the typical constitutional nature of the cooperation. A relevant case is constituted by *First Electric Cooperative* (www.firstelectric.coop) that operates in Arkansas. Founded in 1937, this is a cooperative that provides electric power and now serves over 87,000 customers. In order to get into the cooperative, customers have to pay an admission fee that will be given back to them in case they lose their status of members. Members have the right to receive electric supply and to participate in the annual members' meeting. In the Board, composed of 9 members, local provided districts are represented according to population density.

Though in Italy in the last decades we have assisted to an important development of the non profit sector, through relevant experiences of collaboration with the public administration in the field of public services management, there are no examples similar to those mentioned above. It must be noted that the "non profit phenomenon" is not only dimensionally increasing, but it is also a business development. This "entrepreneurship process" has known an important legal phase with the introduction, in the Italian legal order, of the social cooperatives' law, and few years later, of the social enterprise's law (D. Lgs. 155/2006). With the latter, the spirit of solidarity of NPOs can be strengthened thanks to an "entrepreneurial matrix" (C. Borzaga/J. Defourny (eds.) 2001: 284; F. Alleva 2007: 55-92; C. Borzaga/L. Fazzi (eds.) 2008: 210-230). In this perspective the social enterprise acquires tools which are typical of profit realities, like professionalism in management and a structured organisation, making it easier to meet their social goals (P.A. Mori 2006: 307-312).

It has to be noted that this new juridical figure has to implement, *ex lege*, participated governance models. To do so, the Italian lawmaker has provided for involved forms of employees and customers, through a participated governance model, formally explicit and with the use of special accountability tools, like the social balance sheet being published. The Italian lawmaker also has given the chance to everybody to implement their own models for the application of participation forms. This is done in view of introducing different typologies of involvement, as adequate as possible to the organisational structures and, consequently, of facilitating the possibility to implement and respect inclusive forms among individuals.

Although this juridical qualification suffers from some imperfections due to its recent introduction in the Italian law system and to the lack of concrete incentives (even of fiscal nature), an interesting prospective of a new interlocutor emerges. In the light of its juridical characteristics, it can be considered as an innovative action model in all those sectors which are characterised by contractual incompleteness and in all those contexts where a safeguard of some groups of "weak" individuals becomes necessary. The use of the social enterprise in the public utilities' sector boosts the promotion of an interesting tool that otherwise would be limited.

8. Some conclusive remarks

This paper offers a possible interpretational framework for the current dynamics in the public sector, highlighting a possible way for experimentations in the field of the management of public services.

It is worth mentioning that the current trend, both in theory and in practice, is to choose hybrid solutions, with the coexistence of elements referred to different conceptual models. Probably those who claim that the one best way does not exist are right, but there are "clothes that should be tailored", in respect of historical, cultural, social, and economical specificities of every context.

The principle of subsidiarity, at the base of a jointly held system in order to offer guarantees and services to the citizens, can unify the need for a renewal with an improvement of the Italian cultural matrix. The adoption of participation mechanisms by citizens can further integrate private parties, thus correcting potential distortions of the pure market principles. The use of NPOs for managing public utilities and especially the social enterprise can be an innovation which can better bridge the gap between demand and supply.

Clearly, these are only first observations that require to be further consolidated through theoretical debate and analyses of experimental practices. That is why the abovementioned international experiences can be considered as initial reference models.

Our point of view aims at overcoming the cyclical debate on the pre-eminence of the State and that of the market. The need to review the Italian welfare system is a stimulus to review the role of the public sector and the forms to relate it to the community. To us, the decisional criterion should be the effectiveness of solutions, and not pre-established ideological positions. Moreover, the most adequate ultimate evaluation should be that of citizens. That is why it is important to have the nerve to experiment, to increase the responsibility assigned to them, and to give them the possibility to choose and control. This is just the beginning of the path.

References

Alford, J./Hughes, O. 2008: Public Value Pragmatism as the Next Phase of Public Management, in: The American Review of Public Administration, n. 38(2), pp. 130-148.

Alleva, F. 2007: L'Impresa Sociale Italiana, Giuffrè, Milano.

Anessi Pessina, E./Steccolini, I. 2005: Evolutions of New Public Management-Inspired Budgeting Practices in Italian Local Governments, in: Public Budgeting & Management, n. 25(2), pp. 1-14.

Ascoli, U. 2003: Le sfide del Non Profit Italiano, in: Non Profit, n. 2, pp. 295-310.

Benington, J. 2009: Creating the Public in Order to Create Public Value?, in: International Journal of Public Administration, n. 32, pp. 232-249.

Bennet, J./Iossa, E./Legrenzi, G. 2003: The Role of Commercial Non-Profit Organizations in the Provision of Public Services, in: Oxford Review of Economic Policy, n. 19(2), pp. 335-347.

Bingham, L./Nabatchi, T./O'Leary, R. 2005: The New Governance: Practices and Processes for Stakeholder and Citizen Participation in the Work of Government, in: Public Administration Review, n. 65(5), pp. 547-558.

Birchall, J. 2002: Mutual, Non-Profit or Public Interest Company? An Evaluation of Options for the Ownership and Control of Water Utilities, in: Annals of Public and Cooperative Economics, n. 73(2), pp. 181-213.

Bishop, P./Davis, G. 2002: Mapping Public Participation in Policy Choices, in: Australian Journal of Public Administration, n. 61(1), pp. 14-29.

Borgonovi, E. 2002: Principi e Sistemi Aziendali per le Amministrazioni Pubbliche, Egea, Milano.

Borzaga, C. 2003: La Legge Delega sull'Impresa Sociale: Riflessioni nella Prospettiva dei Decreti Delegati, in: Impresa sociale, n. 67, pp. 14-28.

Borzaga, C./Fazzi, L. (eds) 2008: Governo e Organizzazione per l'Impresa Sociale, Carocci, Roma.

Borzaga, C./Defourny, J. (eds.) 2001: L'impresa Sociale in Prospettiva Europea, Edizioni 31, Trento.

Brereton, M./Temple, M. 1999: The New Public Service Ethos: An Ethical Environment for Governance, in: Public Administration, n. 77(3), pp. 455-474.

Bressan, E. 2007: Breve Storia della Sussidiarietà, in: G. Vittadini (ed): Che Cosa è la Sussidiarietà. Un Altro Nome della Libertà, Guerini e Associati, Milano.

Brugnoli, A./Vittadini, G. (eds.) 2008: La Sussidiarietà in Lombardia, IRER, Milano.

Brugué, Q./Gallego, R. 2003: A Democratic Public Administration? Developments in Public Participation and Innovation in Community Governance, in: Public Management Review, n. 5(3), pp. 425-447.

Callahan, K. 2007: Citizen Participation: Models and Methods, in: International Journal of Public Administration, n. 30(11), pp. 1179-1196.

Capano, G. 2003: Administrative Traditions and Policy Change: When Policy Paradigms Matter. The Case of Italian Administrative Reform during the 1990s, in: Public Administration, n. 81(4), pp. 781-801.

Cappelletti, D./Mittone, L. 2008: La Crisi del Welfare State e le Organizzazioni Non Profit Multi-stakeholder, in: Impresa Sociale, n. 4, pp. 21-47.

Cepiku, D. 2005: Governance: Riferimento Concettuale o Ambiguità Terminologia nei Processi Innovativi della P.A.?, in: Azienda Pubblica, n. 1, pp. 84-110.

Cepiku, D. 2006: Governance e Istituzioni Internazionali: dalla Definizione alla Misurazione, in: Azienda Pubblica, n. 1, pp. 37-53.

Council of Europe 2001: Recommendation of the Committee of Ministers to Member States on the Participation of Citizens in Local Public Life, n. 19, Bruxelles.

Cuthill, M./Fien, J. 2005: Building Community Capacity Through Citizen Participation in Local Governance, in: Australian Journal of Public Administration, n. 64(4), pp. 63-80.

D'Alessio, L. 1992: La Gestione delle Aziende Pubbliche. Problemi di Programmazione, Controllo e Coordinamento, Giappichelli, Torino.

De Bruijn, H./Dicke, W. 2006: Strategies for Safeguarding Public Values in Liberalized Utility Sector, in: Public Administration, n. 84(3), pp. 717-735.

Denhardt, R. B./Denhardt, J. V. 2000: The New Public Service: Serving Rather Than Steering, in: Public Administration Review, n. 60(6), pp. 549-559.

Denhardt, R. B./Denhardt, J. V. 2002: The New Public Service, Armonk, New York.

Depedri, S. 2008a: The Competitive Advantages of Social Enterprises, in: L. Becchetti / C. Borzaga (eds.), The Economics of Social Responsibility, Carocci, Roma.

Depedri, S. 2008b: La Dimensione Multi-stakeholder delle Cooperative Sociali, in: Impresa Sociale, n. 4, pp. 72-103.

Donati, P. 2004: Il Mercato di Qualità Sociale Come Ambiente e Come Prodotto dell'Economia Civile, in: Quaderni AICCON, n. 1, pp. 23-42.

Dragone, D./Viviani, M. 2008: Cultura Organizzativa e Sostenibilità della Governance Multi-stakeholder, in: Impresa Sociale, n. 4, pp. 163-192.

Elefanti, M. 2003a: La Liberalizzazione dei Servizi Pubblici Locali, Egea, Milano.

Elefanti, M. 2003b: Potenzialità e Limiti nella Liberalizzazione dei Servizi Pubblici Locali, in: Management delle Utilities, n. 3, pp. 27-35.

Elster, J. 1998: Deliberative Democracy, Cambridge University Press, Cambridge.

Entwistle, T./Martin, S. 2005: From Competition to Collaboration in Public Service Delivery: A New Agenda for Research, in: Public Administration, n. 83(1), pp. 233-242.

Farneti, G./Pozzoli, S. 2005: Principi e Sistemi Contabili negli Enti Locali. Il Panorama Internazionale, Le Prospettive in Italia, Franco Angeli, Milano.

Fazzi, L. 2000: La Riforma dell'Assistenza in Italia e i Quasi Mercati, in: Economia Pubblica, n. 6, pp. 35-71.

Fazzi, L. 2007: Governance per le imprese sociali e il non profit, Carocci, Roma.

Fazzi, L. 2008: Governare un'Impresa Sociale Secondo l'Approccio Multi-stakeholder: un'Analisi di Casi, in: Impresa sociale, n. 4, pp. 193-225.

Ferlie, E./Steane, P. 2002: Changing Developments in NPM, in: International Journal of Public Administration, n. 25, pp. 1459-1469.

Fortuna, F. 2001: Corporate Governance: Soggetti, Modelli e Sistemi, FrancoAngeli, Milano.

Franch, M./Leonardi, E. 2008: La Realizzazione del Modello Multi-stakeholder in una Cooperativa Sociale: il Caso "Stella Montis" di Fondo, in: Impresa sociale, n. 4, pp. 226-238.

Franklin, A. L./Ho, A. T./Ebdon, C. 2009: Participatory Budgeting in Midwestern States: Democratic Connection or Citizen Disconnection? In: Public Budgeting & Finance, n. 29(3), pp. 52-73.

Garrone, P. 2010: Non Profit Utilities: Caratteristiche ed Esperienze Internazionali, in: P. Garrone/P. Nardi (eds), Al Servizio della Persona e della Città, Guerini e Associati, Milano.

Glas Cymru 2009: Policy and Procedure for the Selection and Appointment of the Members of Glas Cymru Cyfyngedig, http://www.dwrcymru.com/_library/leaflets_publications_english/application_forms/glas_cymru_membership/ Policy_Procedures_Members_Appointment_2009.pdf

Hansmann, H. 1996: The Ownership of Enterprise, Harvard University Press, Cambridge.

Haque, M. S. 2000: Significance of Accountability Under the New Approach to Public Governance, in: International Review of Administrative Sciences, n. 66(4), pp. 599-617.

Hartley, T. W. 2006: Public Perception and Participation in Water Reuse, in: Desalination, n. 187, pp. 115-126.

Holtham, G. 1997: The Water Industry: Why it Should Adopt the Mutual Society Model, in: Journal of Co-operative Studies, n. 88, pp. 3-8.

Hood, C. 1991: A Public Management for All Season?, in: Public Administration, n. 69(1), pp. 3-19.

Hood, C. 1995: The New Public Financial Management in the 1980s: Variations on a Theme, in: Accounting, Organizations and Society, n. 20 (2/3), pp. 93-109.

Horner L./Hazel L. (2005), Adding Public Value, The Work Foundation, London, 2005

Johnston, V. R./Seidenstat, P. 2007: Contracting Out Government Services: Privatization at the Millennium, in. International Journal of Public Administration, n. 30, pp. 231-247.

Kay, J. 1996: Regulating Private Utilities: the Customer Corporation, in: Journal of Co-operative Studies, n. 87, pp. 28-46.

Kelly, G./Mulgan, G./Muers, S. 2002: Creating Public Value: an Analytical Framework for Public Service Reform, Discussion paper prepared by the Cabinet Office Strategy Unit, United Kingdom.

Kickert, W. 1997: Public Governance in Netherlands: An alternative to Anglo-American "managerialism", in: Public Administration, n. 75(4), pp. 731-752.

Kluvers, R./Pillay, S. 2009: Participation in the Budgetary Process in Local Government, in: Australian Journal of Public Administration, n. 68(2), pp. 220-230.

Kooiman, J. 1999: Social- Political Governance: Levels, Models and Orders of Social-Political Interaction, in. Public Management Review, n. 1.

Kuhlmann, S. 2010: New Public Management for the "Classical Continental European Administration": Modernization at the Local Level in Germany, France and Italy, in: Public Administration, n. 88(4), pp. 1116-1130.

Le Grand, J. 1990: Quasi Market and Social Policy, in: The Economic Journal, n. 101, pp. 1256-1267.

Maino, G. 2008: Il Dialogo con gli Interlocutori nelle Imprese Cooperative Sociali, in: Impresa sociale, n. 4, pp. 125-162.

Mayntz, R. 1999: La Teoria della Governance: Sfide e Prospettive, in. Rivista Italiana di Scienza della Politica, n. 29(1), pp. 3-22.

Megginson, W./Netter, J. 2001: From State to Market: a Survey of Empirical Studies on Privatization, in: Journal of Economic Literature, n. 39(2), pp. 321-389.

Meneguzzo, M. 1995: Dal New Public Management alla Public Governance: il Pendolo della Ricerca sulla Pubblica Amministrazione, in: Azienda Pubblica, n. 3, pp. 491-510.

Meneguzzo, M. 1997: Ripensare la Modernizzazione Amministrativa e il New Public Management. L'Esperienza Italiana: Innovazione dal Basso e Sviluppo della Governance Locale, in: Azienda Pubblica, n. 4, pp. 587-608.

Minogue, M. 2000: Should Flawed Models of Public Management be Exported? Issues and Practice. Working Paper No. 15, Institute for Development Policy and Management, University of Manchester

Miranda, R./Lerner, A. 1995: Bureaucracy, Organizational Redundancy and the Privatization of Public Services, in: Public Administration Review, n. 55(2), pp. 193-200.

Moore, M. 1995: Creating Public Value, Cambridge, MA: Harvard University Press.

Mori, P. A. 2006: Alcune Riflessioni su Natura e Motivazioni Economiche dell'Impresa Sociale, in: Non profit, n. 2, pp. 307-312.

Morse, L. B. 2000: A Case for Water Utilities as Cooperative and the UK Experience, in: Annals of Public and Cooperative Economics, n. 71(3), pp. 467-495.

Mussari, R. 1994: Il Management delle Aziende Pubbliche. Profili Teorici, Cedam, Padova.

Mussari, R. 1997: Autonomy, Responsibility and New Public Management in Italy, in: L. R. Jones/K. Schedler/S. W. Wade (eds.): Advances in International Comparative Management. International Perspectives on the New Public Management, Greenwich-Connecticut, Jai Press Inc.

Novy, A./Leubolt, B. 2005: Participatory Budgeting in Porto Alegre: Social Innovation and the Dialectical Relationship of State and Civil Society, in: Urban Studies, n. 42(11), pp. 2023-2036.

O'Flynn, J. 2007: Form New Public Management to Public Value: Paradigmatic Change and Managerial Implications, in: The Australian Journal of Public Administration, n. 66(3), pp. 353-366.

OECD 2001: Citizens as Partners: Information, Consultation and Public Participation in Policy Making, OECD Publications, Paris.

Peters, B. G. (2008): Debate: The Two Futures of Public Administration, in: Public Money & Management, n. 8, pp. 195-196.

Pollitt, C./Bouckaert, G. 2002: La Riforma del Management Pubblico, Università Bocconi Editore, Milano.

Prasad, N. 2006: Privatisation Results: Private Sector Participation in Water Services After 15 Years, in: Development Policy Review, n. 24(6), pp. 669-692.

Putnam, R. 2005: A New Movement for Civic Renewal, in: Public Management, n. 7, pp. 7-10.

Rhodes, R./Wanna, J. 2007: The Limits to Public Value, or Rescuing Responsible Government from the Platonic Guardians, in: The Australian Journal of Public Administration, n. 66(4), pp. 406-421.

Rhodes, R. 1996: The New Governance: Governing Without Government, in: Political Studies, n. 44(4), pp. 652-667.

Rodger, J. 2000: From a Welfare State to a Welfare Society: the Changing Context of Social Policy in a Post Modern Era, St Martin's Press, New York.

Royo, S./Yetano, A./Acerete, B. 2011: Citizen Participation in German and Spanish Local Governments: a Comparative Study, in: International Journal of Public Administration, n. 34(3), pp. 139-150.

Sacchetti, S./Tortia, E. 2008: Dall'Organizzazione Multi-stakeholder all'Impresa Reticolare, in: Impresa Sociale, n. 4, pp. 104-124.

Sacconi, L. 2005: Ancora sull'Insorgenza dell'Impresa Sociale. La Complementarietà tra Preferenze Conformiste e Ricerca della Reputazione, in: Impresa Sociale, n. 4, pp. 133-156.

Sacconi, L./Faillo, M. 2005: Come Emerge l'Impresa Sociale? Uno Sguardo d'Assieme alla Teoria della Complementarietà tra ideologia , Governance e Accountability, in: Impresa Sociale, n. 4, pp. 82-105.

San Mauro, C. 2004: I Nuovi Strumenti di Regolazione dei Servizi Pubblici: la Carta dei Servizi Pubblici e il Contratto di Servizio, Maggioli, Rimini.

Sancino, A. 2010: Debate: Community Governance as a Response to Economic Crisis, in: Public Money & Management, n. 3, pp. 117-120.

Skelcher, C./Torfing, J. 2010: Improving Democratic Governance Through Institutional Design: Civic Participation and Democratic Ownership in Europe, in: Regulation & Governance, n. 1(4), pp. 71-91.

Smith, R. F. I. 2004: Focusing on Public Value: Something New and Something Old, in: The Australian Journal of Public Administration, n. 63(4), pp. 68-79.

Stoker, G. 2006: Public Value Management: A Narrative for Networked Governance?, in: The American Review of Public Administration, n. 36(1), pp. 41-57.

Taylor, F. W. 1911: The Principles of Sientific Management, Harper, New York.

Terry, L. D. 1998: Administrative Leadership, Neo-managerialism, and the Public Management Movement, in: Public Administration Review, n. 58(3), pp. 194-200.

Thomas, D. 2001: Welsh Water: Role Model or Special Case?, in: Utilities policy, n. 10, pp. 99-114.

UNDP: The Role of Participation and Partnership in Decentralized Governance: A Brief Synthesis of Policy Lessons and Recommendation of Nine Country Case Studies on Service Delivery for the Poor, *www.undp.org/governance*.

Vigoda, E. 2002: From Responsiveness to Collaboration: Governance, Citizens, and the Next Generation of Public Administration, in: Public Administration Review, n. 62(5), pp. 527-540.

Vittadini, G. 2007: Che Cosa è la Sussidiarietà, Guerini e Associati, Milano.

Viviani, M. 2006: Il Coinvolgimento degli Stakeholder nelle Organizzazioni Socialmente Responsabili, Maggioli, Rimini.

Wilson, W. 1887: The Study of Administration, in: Political Science Quarterly, n. 2, pp. 197-222.

World Bank 1997: World Development Report: the State in a Changing World, Washington, D.C.

World Bank 2004: World Development Report: Making Services Work for Poor People, Oxford University Press, Oxford.

Young, D. R. 2001: Organizational Identity in Nonprofit Organizations: Strategic and Structural Implications, in: Nonprofit Management and Leadership, n. 12, pp. 139-157.

Zamagni, S. (ed.) 1998: Non Profit Come Economia Civile, Il Mulino, Bologna.

Zangrandi, A. 1994: Autonomia ed Economicità nelle Aziende Pubbliche, Giuffrè, Milano.

EMBEDDED SYSTEMS IN THE EUROPEAN METROPOLITAN REGION OF NUREMBERG – A CLUSTER DEVELOPMENT ANALYSIS

CHRISTIAN SCHEINER / CHRISTIAN BACCARELLA /
STEPHAN HOHENADL / KAI-INGO VOIGT
(UNIVERSITY ERLANGEN-NUREMBERG, GERMANY)

1. Introduction

The progressing globalization and concomitant advantages seem to push the significance of site selection as a competitive factor further into the background. However, at a closer look, the opposite turns out to be the case. Site selection is becoming increasingly global, but companies focus the desired know-how and search for sites close to industry competitors more than ever (Späth 2003; Porter 2000). This encourages the formation of clusters, which succeeded in gaining the attention of scientists from different fields over the last years. Numerous research projects and analyses of clusters worldwide led to the conclusion that they not only foster productivity and innovation within companies, but also facilitate the foundation of new firms (e.g. Späth 2003; Porter 1998, 2000, Schiele 2003, Martin & Sunley 2003; Rosenfeld 1997; Cooke & Huggins 2003; van den Berg et al 2001, Cooke 2001; Marshall 1956).

The European Metropolitan Region Nuremberg (EMN) in Germany ranks among the nation's top locations. This is especially reflected by the high density of patents and founding activities within the metropolitan area. A large number of companies dealing with embedded systems accrued in the metropolitan region of Nuremberg over the last few years.

Embedded systems are designated as the key technology of the 21st century (Heng 2001) and are expected to experience an immense growth as by now they are the driving force behind numerous product innovations. The purpose of this study is the derivation of indicators about the behavior of companies in the field of embedded systems in order to gain insights into the cluster formation in the EMN. Therefore an empirical study was conducted with the focus on the examination of cooperative relations between companies and the Marshall externalities, which are a special characteristic in clusters. The questionnaire was answered by 123 companies, which results in a response rate of 10%.

2. Embedded Systems

The term „embedded system" refers to an information-processing system that is embedded in a product, which itself appears not to be a computer (Simon 1999). There, it performs complex tasks of control, regulation and monitoring of technical, physical, chemical or biological processes and can also be used for the operation and visualisation of automation processes and as an interface to remote systems (Broy et al. 1998).

Typically, most embedded systems have no mouse, no keyboard and no big screens as user interfaces, but use a need-based user interface (e.g. buttons, joystick) (Marwedel 2007; Scholz 2005). For this reason, such systems disappear in the background and are hardly noticed by users. Many authors also unite them under the general phrase „disappearing computer" (Mattern 2005; Russel et al. 2005).

Unlike a general-purpose personal computer, embedded systems are highly specialised and designed for just one specific task. They usually perform safety- and time-critical tasks (Marwedel 2007), such as the airbag control in motor vehicles or the anti-collision system in aircrafts. They appear in many areas of our everyday life. They are particularly used in the automotive industry (e.g. ABS), air travel industry (e.g. autopilot), railways (e.g. braking systems), telecommunications, medical technology (e.g. pacemakers), and electronics (e.g. DVD players) (Marwedel 2007, Scholz 2005). Because of the breadth of their applications in different industries, embedded systems are considered a cross-section technology, which is open to different usages.

The importance of embedded systems is enormous and can be illustrated from a number of perspectives. Embedded systems are used on a broad front in all areas of technology and have a significant share of the value of many modern products. For example, as estimated by the German Federal Association for Information Technology, Telecommunications and New Media, the proportion of products which include embedded systems is about 80% of the total added value of the processing industries (BITKOM 2007). More than nine out of ten of all electronic components and parts will be implemented in embedded systems and more than 99% of worldwide produced processors are built into embedded systems (Turley 1999).

The market volume of the hardware and the software, used worldwide for the production of embedded systems, amounted to around 163 billion euro in 2008. However, this does not include the value share which comes from the manufacturers of end-products, in which embedded systems are used (Bonn 2008).

Embedded systems are also called the key technology of the 21st Century (Heng 2001) and are, by now, the driving force behind product innovations (Garbers 2007). Today up to 90% of all innovations in the automotive industry have resulted from the electronics embedded in motor vehicles.

3. European Metropolitan Region of Nuremberg

3.1 Background and concept definition

The term "metropolitan area" was introduced in the early 1930's in the USA, serving both as statistical reference to spatial development and, more importantly, to represent the spatial units formed by suburbanization in a better way than it was possible by using the existing administrative boundaries (Adam & Göddecke-Stellman 2002). Metropolitan regions describe "spatial and functional sites" and "radiate their outstanding functions in international aspect across national borders". "As engines of public, economic, social and cultural development, they should support the performance ability and the competitiveness of Germany and Europe, thus contributing to the acceleration of the European integration process" (MKRO Decision 1995).

Unlike other European countries, where a single metropolitan region is dominant, such as Paris in France and London in England, Germany is characterised by a system of various metropolitan regions, which has a decisive influence on Germany's competitiveness in the global economy (Kujath et al. 2002). There are no uniform definitions regarding the size of metropolitan regions and their demarcation to other regions. The spatial concentration of the metropolitan functions plays a decisive role in the demarcation (Blotevogel 2002).

3.2 Metropolitan functions

Metropolitan regions are political and economic decision making centres, in which global financial and information flows are controlled. In a metropolitan region there are many national and international businesses, financial centres and public institutions, which, on the one hand, exert a gravitational power on businesses and, on the other hand, give the cities and the regions a cross-regional radiation (Adam 2006). While the public sector is not as strongly engaged as in other regions, in the private sector some leading companies have located their headquarters or at least major offices in the metropolitan region. The EMN belongs to Europe's top IT locations and possesses top class competences, especially in the field of the promising technologies of the future. Among the largest and strongest companies are there global players such as *Siemens*, *Adidas*, *GfK*, *Bosch*, *Diehl*, *Ina Schaeffler*, *MAN* or more national-focused companies like *DATEV*, *N-Ergie* and *Nürnberger Versicherung*.

Metropolitan regions are centres of innovation, which, in addition to knowledge, also generate and spread attitudes, values and innovative products. Blotevogel (2002) distinguishes between (a) economic-technical innovations and (b) social and cultural innovations. The presence of these two groups creates the necessary climate for innovation, knowledge transfer and cooperation, and thus forms the key to economic growth and competitiveness in a metropolitan region.

In our metropolitan region, the innovation and competition function is marked mainly by the schools and the internationally renowned research institutions existing there, for there are six universities and ten polytechnics in the EMN. Even as far as the research and application centres are concerned, the EMN is diversified. The structurally stable mix of small and medium-sized companies and global players with their own research facilities also supports the growth of knowledge and know-how.

The gateway function describes the access to people, knowledge and markets. Metropolitan regions are important traffic junctions and have developed an optimally built infrastructure. Another important feature of the gateway function is the presence of different media (e.g. television or fairs).

The EMN has an excellent infrastructure network for automobiles/ trucks, planes, trains and boats and is distinguished by its central location in the pan-European economic space. Four of the main European highways (in Germany numbered A3, A6, A7 and A9) cross the metropolitan region, thus forming an important traffic intersection. With traffic of more than 13 million tons in 2007, the Nuremberg port is a central hub between the North Sea port of Rotterdam and the South Eastern European Danube ports to the Black Sea. Moreover, it is the largest multifunctional transport and logistics centre in Southern Germany (Wirtschaftsbericht 2007). With its volume of over 4 million passengers, the Nuremberg airport is among the smaller airports in Germany, nevertheless, it has great significance for the metropolitan region.

Another important aspect of the gateway function is the access to knowledge and markets. The *Nürnberger Messe* is, above all, of outstanding importance for the access to markets and ranks among the top 10 exhibition venues in Europe and among the 15 largest in the world.

3.3 Profile of the European Metropolitan Region of Nuremberg

The EMN is divided into a core area and the surrounding metropolitan network. The core area consists of 8 district-free cities and 12 administrative districts, which are closely intertwined with each other. The core area centres around the city axis of Erlangen-Nuremberg-Fürth-Schwabach. The closely and diversely intertwined metropolitan core is complemented by other cities and areas that form the network of the metropolitan region.

With 3.5 million inhabitants, 1.8 million workers, over 150,000 companies, 50,000 self-employed and a GDP of 103 billion euro in 2007, the

EMN belongs to one of the strongest economic regions in Europe (Prast 2008).

The development model of the EMN presents six core technological competences and one cross-section competence in a focal point. These competences are characterised by high growth potentials which provide the metropolitan region with strength above the average levels (Entwicklungsleitbild 2005). These are information and communication, transport and logistics, medicine and health, energy and environment, new materials, automation and production technology, and innovative services.

4. Cluster theory

4.1 Definition and characteristics

Within the scientific literature a multitude of different definitions for a cluster can be found. Swann and Prevezer (1996) define clusters as "groups of firms within one industry based in one geographical area" (p. 139). For Rosenfeld (1997) clusters are "a geographically bounded concentration of interdependent businesses with active channels for business transactions, dialogue and communications, that collectively shares common opportunities and threats" (p. 10). Porter, in contrast, defines a cluster as "a geographic concentration of interconnected companies and institutions in a given sector. It includes a number of networked branches and other organisation units relevant to the competition. [...] Finally, many clusters include state and other institutions such as universities, standard-setting bodies, think tanks, educational institutions and commercial organizations, which provide special education and training, information, research and technical support" (Porter 1998, p. 77).

Although these definitions differ in many aspects, each of them is based on the two common characteristics:

- that companies in an industry or from related industries must be geographically concentrated in a cluster (geographical dimension),
- and that they have to be connected in some way with each other (functional dimension).

Besides the geographical and functional dimensions, Cooke (2001) also considers the development of a cluster and classifies clusters by various levels of development. Thus, clusters can be distinguished into three different characteristic forms:

- The weakest form of a cluster, "the aspiring cluster", includes only agglomerations of companies without explicit interactions and synergies between the companies.
- In a "latent cluster" the companies are already beginning to gain profit from the sporadically occurring positive effects of the geographical proximity. Much of the potential for interaction and coop-

eration and the results from those synergies are, however, not yet used.

• "Working clusters" can fully use their potentials, since the individual companies form a collective system, in which the interactions and the collaborations between the companies and other relevant institutions in geographical proximity are strongly expressed and all parties involved benefit from that (Cooke 2001; Rosenfeld 1997).

Within this work we will use the following definition based on Porter: A cluster is a collection of geographically concentrated and located nearby business and business-related institutions (such as research and development institutions, government agencies), acting on the same or related final product markets along the value chain. These companies and institutions show different and complementary knowledge in connection to a specific aspect of product, service or production, compete with each other and at the same time cooperate with each other (Porter 1998).

4.2 Concepts for explaining cluster formation

The concept of industrial districts was originally coined by the British economist Alfred Marshall. In his work he examined regional production networks of small and medium enterprises and by using the term industrial district, he meant "the geographic concentration of firms from a given industry, which develops dynamically on the basis of external effects and location advantages" (Maier & Tödtling 2002; Marshall 1956). He attributed the formation of industrial districts specifically to labour market effects, industry specialisation as well as to knowledge spillover effects. The formation of clusters can, thus, be retroactively explained on the basis of industrial structures and effect relationships that were observed in the growth and maturation phase of an industry (Krafft 2006). Therefore, the concept of industrial districts and, in particular, the described Marshall externalities play an important role in the explanation of clusters, since these Marshall externalities increase the incentive to spatial concentration of businesses, educational institutions, research and development facilities and institutions, and thus are characteristic of a cluster (Hafner 2008).

Marshall's concept of industrial districts was picked up in the early 1980s by Italian and American researchers such as Becattini and Brusco and was further developed (Zeitlin 1992). Since the properties of the studied regions reminded very much of the industrial districts described by Marshall, in literature, this concept became also known as "new industrial districts" (Bathelt 1996). Based on the approaches by Marshall, the growth and the performance of the Italian industrial districts were also supported by factors such as "flexible specialisation" (Mossig 2000;

Bathelt & Glückner 2002), "trust and social embeddedness" (Mossig 2000), "institutional density" (Mossig 2000; Bathelt & Glückner 2002) and "cooperation and competition" (Becattini 1989; Krafft 2006). The main criticism of the concept regarded its representativeness and generalisability because of the difficult transferability to other regions as well as the insufficient study of the economic efficiency of a district (Maier & Tödtling 2002; Schamp 2000). However, the "new industrial district" approach shows a number of strengths and is considered the best-grounded and the most empirically supported concept, because of which it constitutes an important basis for many newer concepts (Krafft 2006).

4.3 Methods for identification and analysis of clusters

In the relevant literature, a variety of methods and approaches exist for the identification and analysis of clusters. The various methods differ in their focus because of the theoretical background, the underlying data and the analysis as well as the applicability to specific case studies. The different methods can be divided into three different levels of analysis, which are depicted in Table 1.

Table 1: Tools for identification and analysis of clusters

Levels of analysis	Objectives	Methods
Macro level	Identification of clusters	Analysis of secondary data
	Spatial and sectoral concentration Sectoral integration Dynamics of the regional economy	Calculation of concentration measures Input-output analysis Portfolio diagram, shift analysis
Meso level	Expertise for identification and analysis of clusters	Survey from cluster experts
	Collecting evidence about cluster assumptions, identification of elements and actors of regional value chains	Expert interviews, participatory methods with the use of creativity and presentation techniques
Micro level	Analysis of clusters	Survey from cluster actors
	Individual elements of regional value chains, transaction and communication linkages	Standardised surveys and qualitative interviews, functions and network analysis

Source: According to Sautter (Regionale Cluster 2004), p. 68.

5. Methodical approach

The analysis of the potential cluster in the field of embedded systems in the European Metropolitan Region of Nuremberg was conducted on the micro level by means of a quantitative inquiry, as a standardised online questionnaire was used. For this purpose, a total of 1235 companies in the metropolitan region were contacted via email and were asked to fill in the questionnaire.

The structure of the questionnaire can be divided into two parts: a general part for acquiring the company-specific characteristics and a thematic part for answering the central research questions. The thematic part was used in order to find an answer to the central research questions. In the centre were the question blocks about the Marshall externalities (specialised suppliers, labour market effects, knowledge spillovers) and about the cooperation behaviour of enterprises. It was also of interest since when the company dealt with embedded systems and what motives they had to do so. Finally, the companies were asked about the importance of different location factors for the competitiveness of the enterprises and about the realisation of these factors through the European Metropolitan Region of Nuremberg.

The data collection of the survey covered a time-period of almost two months. The questionnaire was fully answered by 123 companies. The vast majority of the questionnaires was filled out by directors and executives and more than half of the respondents had worked in the enterprises for more than seven years. As a result of that, a high veracity of the responses could be assumed, since these respondents have profound insight knowledge.

6. Results

6.1 General information

Year of establishment

Most companies were founded between the years of 2001 and 2007. The second largest group consisted of companies that were established between 1991 and 2000. 14% of the companies were founded between 1981 and 1990, 6% between 1971 and 1980, and 11% were established between 1895 and 1970.

Application areas

Frequent mentions regarding application areas included telecommunications (34%), the automotive sector (31%) and medical systems (29%). 26% of the companies were dealing with factory control and 22% with building techniques. Robotics and authentication systems were named by 10% of the companies. The smallest percentage had the sectors railway equipment (9%), aircraft equipment (8%) and military applications (5%). Inter alia, the sectors of plant engineering, electrical engineering, mechanical engineering, electronics and food industries were mentioned as further application areas. More than half of the surveyed companies (53%) produced their goods and services not only for one but for several applications.

Value chain

The value chain for embedded systems can be divided into six levels:
(1) On the first level, there are the chip manufacturers, developing chips and processors for embedded systems.
(2) The second level includes the distributors, who trade in chips, processors and other components from different manufacturers and perform exclusively classical distribution functions.
(3) The board manufacturers combine the various components into functional and mostly application-specific embedded systems.
(4) Then the system/software integrators bring the hardware to life through operating systems and application-specific software.
(5) On the fifth level, there are the device manufacturers, who integrate the embedded systems into their products, so that they take over tasks of controlling, regulating, monitoring and networking.
(6) At the end of the value chain, there are the end users, who modify the finished products and integrate them into their own products or use them in their businesses.

The system/software integrators form the value chain level with the most companies in the EMN. Out of the total of 55 companies on this level, two are in the hardware sector, 24 in the software sector and there are 29 companies in both, the hardware and the software sector. Then the equipment manufacturers follow with a total of 36 companies, the end users with 20 and the board manufacturers with 17 companies. The value chains with the fewest companies are formed by the distributors and the chip manufacturers, which are active in 11 respectively 8 out of the total of 91 companies.

Around 38% of the companies serve on several levels of the value chain. Most surveyed companies are hybrids from system/software integrators and device manufacturers as well as board/equipment manufacturers and system/software integrators. Three companies could also be identified to cover all levels of the value chain. Being asked the question to which areas they can additionally be classified, 60% of the companies responded that they are active both in the hardware and the software sector. 32% worked solely in the software sector and only 8% exclusively in the hardware sector.

Employees

Figure 1 shows the distribution of companies by number of employees. Here, the micro enterprises (1-9 employees) are represented most strongly by a share of 50%. For the companies surveyed, the average growth rate between 2005 and 2008 was in the size class from 6 to 10%.

Figure 1: Number of employees

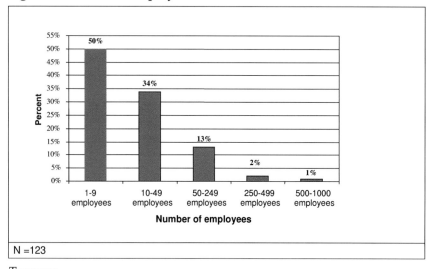

N =123

Turnover

The majority of the companies generated a turnover of less than 500,000 euro. 20% of the companies achieved sales in the range between 500,000 and one million euro, 12% between one and two million euro and 20% of the companies were between two and ten million euro. 10 percent, respectively 2 percent of the surveyed companies were in the top-selling classes (10-50 million EUR, over 50 million EUR). Similar to employment growth, the average growth rates during the last three years turned out to be very different. The results show that 24 companies had an average growth rate between 6% and 10% and 23 companies had a growth rate between 11% and 25%. Eight companies reported that their sales had developed an average of 76% to 100% over the past three years and nine companies had a very high growth of over 100%.

However, there were also eight companies whose sales declined in the last three years. The median of the average turnover growth rates between the years of 2005 and 2008 was in the class from 11% to 25%.

Research and development

Table 2 shows the R&D expenses for hardware and software development in relation to turnover. The median value lies in the second size class – the class from 6 to 10%.

Table 2: Share of R&D expenditure

Class	Absolute (relative) frequency	
	Hardware development	Software development
Share of 1 to 5%	10 (27%)	11 (19%)
Share of 6 to 10%	14 (38%)	16 (28%)
Share of 11 to 15%	4 (11%)	8 (14%)
Share of 16 to 20%	3 (8%)	7 (12%)
Share of 21 to 25%	1 (3%)	5 (9%)
Share of more than 25%	5 (14%)	10 (18%)
Total	37 (100%)	57 (100%)
n =109		

6.2 Information about the object of research – Marshall externalities

The described knowledge spillovers, the specialisation of suppliers and the labour market effects play a significant role in the explanation of clusters (Hafner 2008). Therefore, the characteristics of Marshall externalities are discussed in more detail in the next sections.

Information and knowledge

A positive effect of spatial industry agglomeration, respectively of a cluster, can be made visible in the presence of localised knowledge spillovers, either by the physical proximity to academic institutions, competitors, upstream and downstream companies and customers, or by the informal flow of information in the cluster (Marshall 1956). Therefore, the companies were asked what importance customers, suppliers, competitors, universities/colleges and other research and development institutions had as an external source of knowledge for their innovation abilities. The surveyed companies were provided with a five-point scale, on which to mark their tendencies on the question whether customers, companies and academic institutions within or outside the EMN turned out to be more important as external knowledge sources for the innovation in the company[1].

---

[1] External knowledge sources: "1" = most important sources within the metropolitan area, "3" = equal importance, "5" = most important sources outside the metropolitan area.

Table 3 gives an overview of the companies' assessments when asked about the importance of geographical proximity to external sources of knowledge. From the results it is apparent that, for most surveyed companies, customers, suppliers, competitors, universities, technical colleges and other R&D facilities in the metropolitan region and outside the metropolitan region have the same significance as external knowledge sources. But if one considers the mean values, it becomes clear that, with regard to customers, suppliers, competitors and other R&D facilities as an external source of knowledge for innovation ability, the respondents rather prefer those knowledge sources from outside the metropolitan region.

Table 3: Importance of the geographical proximity to external sources of knowledge

	within the metropolitan region			outside the metropolitan region		
External source of knowledge	very impor- tant	impor- tant	equally impor- tant	impor- tant	very impor- tant	Mean value
Customers (n =70)	21%	7%	40%	9%	23%	3.04
Suppliers (n =67)	10%	8%	61%	5%	16%	3.09
Competitors (n =65)	6%	11%	46%	12%	25%	3.38
Universities/ colleges (n =58)	12%	16%	60%	3%	9%	2.81
Other R&D facilities (n =58)	5%	10%	69%	5%	10%	3.05

Only as far as scientific institutions were concerned, the companies showed higher preferences for the universities and colleges in the metropolitan region as an external knowledge source.

Input

Another positive effect of a cluster is that, due to a sufficiently large demand for materials and intermediate products, a vertically supported branch arises in close spatial proximity. These suppliers show a higher degree of specialisation than distant supplier companies and also offer the possibility to provide fast short-term necessities (Marshall 1956). In the conducted survey, it was of interest what types of inputs the companies integrated into their own products/services, what share of their input the companies purchased from suppliers in the EMN in the last financial year and, especially, how high the degree of specialisation of products and services from suppliers in the EMN was.

Figure 2 shows the answers to the question what kind of inputs the companies obtained: Over half of the surveyed companies integrated communication systems and interfaces from suppliers into their products and have their firmware and operating system software produced by outside companies. 43% of the companies obtained development services in the sector of hardware and 38% got control and operating software from suppliers for their products. Just under a quarter of the companies used results from cooperation with universities and colleges, 21 percent consulting services and 7 percent profits from other research institutions.

Figure 2: Type of input

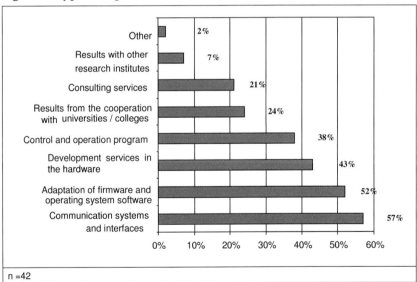

n =42

Table 4 shows the distribution of the companies regarding the question what share of input the companies obtained in the last financial year from suppliers in the European Metropolitan Region of Nuremberg. It is striking that a relatively large part of the respondents (42%) claimed to have received no input from suppliers within the region.

Table 4: Share of the input from the metropolitan region

Class	Absolute frequency	Relative frequency	
Share of 0%	19	42%	
Share of 1 to 10%	16	36%	
Share of 11 to 20%	6	13%	
Share of 21 to 30%	2	4%	
Share of 31 to 40%	1	2%	
Share of 91 to 100%	1	2%	
Total	45	(100)	
n =45			

Regarding the level of input specialisation, the surveyed companies could assess the input from suppliers, which were residents within and outside the metropolitan region, using a five-point scale (1=highly specialised, 5=not specialised). The average values confirmed the thesis, asserted by Marshall and also spread in recent scientific discussions of cluster theory, that a specialised supplier industry arises in a cluster, since the surveyed companies estimated the input from the supply companies in the EMN as relatively specialised (with a mean value of 2.29).[2] However, the companies also considered the suppliers outside the metropolitan region as relatively specialised and even estimated their degree of specialisation as slightly higher (with a mean of 2.12).

Labour market

The third positive effect of a cluster is that through the concentration of an industry in one location, a labour market is formed, which offers a high number of employees with industry-specific qualifications. This exerts strong attraction for both employees and employers. Companies can quickly cover their needs for qualified workers from the regional labour market and save search costs. Besides, qualified workers have better chances of employment because of the high demand (Marshall 1956). That is why the companies were asked to assess the importance of the geographic proximity of enterprises and educational institutions in the

---

[2] The closer to the average value 1, the companies assess the input as more specialized; the closer to the average value 5, the companies assess the input as not so specialized (n =34).

recruitment of their R&D staff. The response options were arranged along a five-point scale[3]. Table 5 shows the results for this question.

Table 5: Importance of the geographic proximity of enterprises and facilities for the process of staff recruitment

	within the metropolitan region			outside the metropolitan region		
Facilities/ companies	very im- portant	important	equally important	important	very im- portant	Mean value
Vocational schools (n=56)	34%	5%	59%	-	2%	2.3
Colleges (n=60)	32%	10%	53%	2%	3%	2.35
Universities (n=59)	27%	15%	49%	3%	5%	2.44
Suppliers (n=57)	9%	14%	63%	4%	11%	2.93
Customers (n=60)	12%	10%	52%	7%	20%	3.13
Competitors (n=53)	9%	8%	57%	8%	19%	3.19
Other companies (n=50)	2%	6%	76%	2%	14%	3.2

Most of the surveyed companies assessed the companies, the educational institutions and the customers within and outside the EMN as equally important with regards to the recruitment of R&D staff. However, it is noticeable that educational institutions in particular, such as vocational schools, colleges and universities in the metropolitan region, are more important for the companies in the recruitment of their R&D employees, than the educational institutions outside the metropolitan region.

Cooperations

Cooperations are the key to economic growth and competitiveness of enterprises, because they facilitate knowledge transfer and encourage the joint creation of new knowledge between companies and academic institutions. Therefore, the cooperation is an essential condition for a functioning and competitive cluster (Cooke 2001; Becattini 1989). That is why companies were asked in which areas they form cooperations, with what partners they cooperate and what objectives they follow through these collaborations. However, the focus of the survey regarding cooperation

---

[3] See FN 1.

behaviour of the companies laid on the question of the origin of the co-operation partners.

From the 74 responding companies, 57% entered within their field of activity in collaborations in the sector of embedded systems. In this aspect, 68% of the companies consider joint research and development and 59% the information exchange with other companies as particularly interesting areas (see Figure 3). The companies are least cooperating with each other in purchasing.

Figure 3: Areas of cooperation

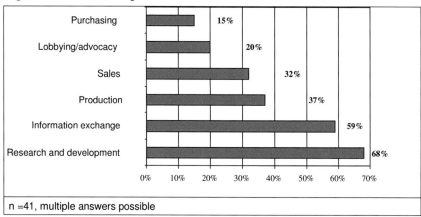

n =41, multiple answers possible

As for the cooperation partners, the companies are focusing more on companies that operate in the same industry (see Figure 4). The acquisition of knowledge, the know-how transfer (78%) and the market access (71%) were reported as the main objectives. It was particularly interesting that 46% of the surveyed enterprises pointed out the importance of ensuring the availability of qualified workers. In addition, the companies cooperate for the purpose of acquiring problem-solving skills (37%), pooling of material resources (34%) and the diversification of their product portfolio (32%).

Figure 4: Cooperation partners

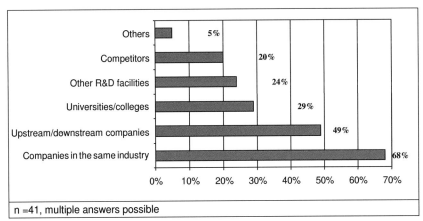

n =41, multiple answers possible

As far as the origin of the cooperation partners is concerned, the companies were asked from what environment the most important cooperation partners and the most numerous cooperation partners came. Here, the question how many of the partners came from the EMN was of special interest. Table 6 provides information about the origin of the most important cooperation partners. It is evident that most companies state that their most important cooperation partners come from Germany, no matter whether these are competitors, companies in the same industry, universities and technical colleges, etc.

Regarding the question from where the majority of the partners came, the responses showed a similar result as the one to the question about the most important cooperation partners. Again, the greatest part of the cooperation partners came from Germany, no matter what partners these were (see Table 6).

Summarising the results, we can state that both the majority and the most important cooperation partners came from Germany; then followed universities, colleges and R&D facilities from the metropolitan region. The upstream and downstream companies in the metropolitan area were mentioned in very few answers. It was also observed that, with regard to the question of the origin of most of the partners, the companies cooperate mostly with competitors, companies in the same industry and upstream and downstream companies from abroad.

Table 6: Origin of the most important and the most numerous partners (numerically)

	Origin							
	from the metropolitan region		from Bavaria		from Germany		from abroad	
Cooperation partner	W	Z	W	Z	W	Z	W	Z
Competitors (n=35)	20%	23%	14%	13%	49%	39%	17%	26%
Companies in the same sector (n=33)	15%	20%	18%	13%	49%	43%	18%	23%
Universities/colleges (n=31)	23%	25%	19%	18%	48%	46%	10%	11%
Other R & D facilities (n=25)	24%	29%	16%	21%	52%	42%	8%	8%
Upstream and down-stream companies (n=29)	10%	8%	24%	23%	45%	46%	21%	23%

W=most important cooperation partners Z =most numerous cooperation partners

Location factors

The next section focuses on the importance of different location factors for the competitiveness of the companies and the realisation through the metropolitan region. It provides an assessment of the relative competitive advantages and location deficits. Bearing the set purpose in mind, the companies were asked to assess the importance of location factors and the realisation of these through the metropolitan region using a five-point scale[4]. Moreover, the companies were asked how they assess the importance of these factors with regard to the future. Again, an underlying five-point scale was used[5].

In the assessment of location factors for competitiveness, the respondents particularly pointed out the availability of qualified workers (see Table 7). In contrast, the economic climate/the image of the EMN, the business friendliness of the local government, the proximity to customers, partners, suppliers, the proximity to research, education and devel-

---

[4] Ranging from "1" = very important to "5" = completely unimportant or 1 = very good to 5 = poor.
[5] Ranging from "1" = strongly increasing to "5" = strongly decreasing.

opment institutions, and the promotion of R&D were given only medium importance with an average rating. The availability of venture
capital and other support had the lowest impact on the competitiveness
of the surveyed companies.

Table 7: Factors of competitiveness

Location factors	Importance	Realisation
Availability of qualified workers (n=68 or 67)	1.43	2.97
Availability of venture capital (n=66 or 50)	3.20	3.44
Economic climate / image of the EMN (n=65 or 61)	2.78	2.59
Business friendliness of the local government (n=66 or 61)	2.67	2.97
Proximity to customers, partners, suppliers (n=67 or 60)	2.54	2.35
Proximity to research, education and development institutions (n =66 or 57)	2.86	2.19
Support from R&D (n=65 or 53)	2.85	2.91
Other support (n=54 or 38)	3.06	3.21

In Figure 5, the area obtained by the importance of location factors is
put in contrast to the relative attractiveness of the EMN. The grey shaded
area shows the difference between the assessment of the importance of
location factors and the realisation of these factors through the EMN and
thus gives information about the location deficits. It turns out that the
availability of qualified workers shows the biggest difference and in this
way the highest urgency to be improved in the future. Slight differences
are evident in the promotion of R&D, other support, availability of venture capital and the business-friendliness of the local government. As a
whole, the juxtaposition of importance and attractiveness shows that, in
terms of location factors, the metropolitan region is actually relatively
well positioned for businesses in the sector of embedded systems. There
is a large difference only in the availability of qualified labour. Regarding the future importance of these location factors for the competitiveness of the enterprises, the largest increase can be noticed in the availability of qualified workers. All other location factors are given un-
changed or slightly increased importance.

Figure 5: Factors of competitiveness

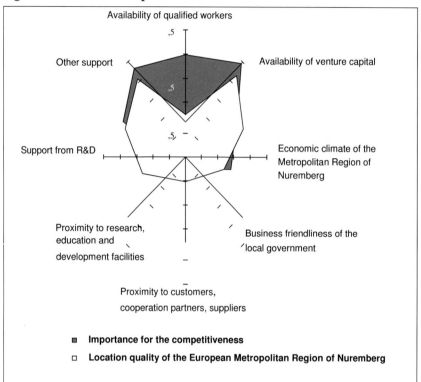

7. Conclusion

The study shows that the Marshall externalities in the metropolitan region are still relatively weakly expressed. Regarding the importance of the geographic proximity to external sources of knowledge, the companies are more likely to prefer customers, suppliers and competitors outside the metropolitan region. As far as the inputs are concerned, the companies assess the products and the services from suppliers in the metropolitan region as relatively specialised. However, most companies obtain only a very small share of their inputs from the metropolitan region. Only the third positive effect of a cluster, the labour market effect, is almost well defined. Nevertheless, the results indicate that there is an enormous gap regarding the importance of qualified workers for the competitiveness of the region and the actual availability of specialized workforce. Companies do seek for personnel in the metropolitan region, but in order to stay competitive, the demand needs to be satisfied. In addition, it must be remembered that a cluster and the effects related to it do not emerge overnight, but take at least 20 years to develop (Porter 2002). Many companies in the European Metropolitan Region of Nuremberg have been active in the field of embedded systems for less than a decade. Therefore, the fact that the European Metropolitan Region of Nuremberg is well positioned with regard to the location factors leads to conclusions about a possible future enhancement of the cluster intensity:

As a whole, it can be concluded that, in the area of embedded systems in the European Metropolitan Region of Nuremberg, a latent and thus emerging cluster seems to exist. To increase the future development potential in the field of embedded systems, sustainable institutions, such as the Open Source Business Foundation or the Embedded Systems Institute, should strengthen the cooperative relations and encourage the interactions in the metropolitan region. Enhancing the educational policy in the field of embedded systems in the European Metropolitan Region of Nuremberg should also be considered to further strengthen the growth of the emerging cluster. Recent efforts and activities show that the development of a cluster is driven forward by adequate means and so a positive development is observed.

References

Adam, Brigitte (2006): Europäische Metropolregionen in Deutschland – Perspektiven für das nächste Jahrzehnt, in: Konrad-Adenauer-Stiftung e.V. (eds.): Materialien für die Arbeit vor Ort, No. 34, Sankt Augustin.

Adam, Brigitte; Göddecke-Stellmann, Jürgen (2002): Metropolregionen – Konzepte, Definitionen und Herausforderungen, in: Informationen zur Raumentwicklung, No. 9, pp. 513-525.

Bathelt, Harald; Glückner, Johannes (2002): Wirtschaftsgeographie – Ökonomische Beziehungen in räumlicher Perspektive, Stuttgart.

Becattini, Giacomo (1998): Les districts industriels en Italie, in: Maruani, Magaret; Reynaud, Emmanuèlle; Romani, Claudine (eds.): La flexibilité en Italie - Débats sur l'emploi, Paris, pp. 261-268.

BITKOM – Bundesverband Informationswirtschaft, Telekommunikation und neue Medien e.V. (2007): Studie „Zukunft digital Wirtschaft – Volkswirtschaftliche Bedeutung der ITK-Wirtschaft", in: www.bitkom.org/files/documents/ Zukunft_ digitale_Wirtschaft.pdf, accessed on May 12, 2011.

Blotevogel, Hans Heinrich (2002): Deutsche Metropolregionen in der Vernetzung, in: Informationen zur Raumentwicklung, No. 6/7, pp. 345-351.

Blotevogel Hans Heinrich (2005a): Metropolräume und ländliche Räume – eine Solidaritätsgemeinschaft?, in: Akademie für Raumforschung und Landesplanung (eds.): Leitlinien der niedersächsischen Landespolitik, Hannover, pp. 12-18.

Blotevogel, Hans Heinrich (2005b): Metropolregionen, in: Akademie für Raumforschung und Landesplanung (eds.): Handwörterbuch der Raumordnung, Vol. 2005, 4th Edition, Hannover, pp. 642-647.

Bonn, Heinz Paul (2008): Speech during press-talk regarding Embedded Systems, in: www.bitkom.org/files/documents/BITKOM_Vortrag_Bonn_PK_Embedded_Systems_ 21_04_2008.pdf, accessed on May 19, 2008.

Broy, Manfred; von der Beeck, Michael; Krüger, Ingolf (1998): SOFT-BED: Problemanalyse für ein Großverbundprojekt Systemtechnik Automobil – Software für eingebettete Systeme. Problemanalyse im Auftrag des BMBF.

Burger, Frank (2007): Innere Werte, in: McK Wissen, Vol. 20, pp. 110-113.

Charta der Metropolregion Nürnberg (2005), in: http://www.em-n.eu/ fileadmin/mrn/Downloads/Charta_120505.pdf, accessed on May 15, 2008.

Cooke, Philip (2001): Knowledge Economies – Clusters, Learning and Co-operative Advantage, New York.

Cooke, Philip; Huggins, Robert (2003): High Technology Clustering in Cambridge, in: Sforzi, Fabio (eds.): The Institution of Local Development, Burlington, pp. 51-74.

Entwicklungsleitbild der Wirtschaftsregion Nürnberg (2005), in: http://www. wirtschaft.nuernberg.de/ver2004/decidedownloads/dl/Entwicklungsleit-bild_ 005_99.pdf, accessed on May 6, 2011.

Garbers, Axel (09th July 2007): Vortrag im Rahmen des BITKOM-Workshops „Mobile Motion Tracking Services – Hightech im Sport", ISPO (Munich), in: www.bitkom.org/files/documents/090720_MMTS_Begruessung_Garbers_v5 _final.pdf, accessed on May 16, 2010.

Hafner, Kurt A. (2008): Clusterbildung und die Rolle der Politik – Wie beurteilen deutsche Unternehmen Firmencluster?, in: ifo Schnelldienst, Vol. 61, No. 1, pp. 37-40.

Heng, Stefan (2001): Embedded Systems – Der (verdeckte) Siegeszug einer Schlüsseltechnologie, in: Economics – Internet-Revolution und „New Economy", Vol. 11, No. 2, pp. 1-12.

Krafft, Lutz (2006): Entwicklung räumlicher Cluster – Das Beispiel Internet- und E-Commerce-Gründungen in Deutschland, Wiesbaden.

Krugman, Paul (1991): Geography and Trade, Leuven-Cambridge-London.

Kujath, Hans Joachim; Dybe, Georg; Fichter, Heidi (2002): Europäische Verflechtungen deutscher Metropolräume und Auswirkungen auf die Raumstruktur des Bundesgebietes, Bonn.

Leitbilder und Handlungsstrategien für die Raumentwicklung in Deutschland – Diskussionspapier (2005), in: http://bfag-aring.de/, accessed on 19.05.2008.

Maier, Gunther; Tödtling, Franz (2002): Regional- und Stadtökonomik 2 – Regionalentwicklung und Regionalpolitik, Wien/New York.

Marshall, Alfred (1959): Principles of Economics, London.

Martin, Ron; Sunley, Peter (2003): Deconstructing clusters: chaotic concept or policy panacea?, in: Journal of Economic Geography, Vol. 3, No. 1, pp. 5-35.

Marwedel, Peter (2007): Eingebettete Systeme, Heidelberg.

Mattern, Friedemann (2005): Allgegenwärtige und verschwindende Computer, in: Praxis der Informationsverarbeitung und Kommunikation (PIK), Vol. 28, No. 1, pp. 29-36.

Ministerkonferenz für Raumordnung (MKRO) (1995): Beschluss der Ministerkonferenz – 24. Sitzung, in: http://www.bmvbs.de/cae/servlet/contentblob/58514/publicationFile/29698/ministe rkonferenz-mkro-beschluss-uebersicht-1967-2010.pdf, accessed on Feb. 8, 2010

Moßig, Ivo (2000): Räumliche Konzentration der Verpackungsmaschinenbau-Industrie in Westdeutschland – Eine Analyse des Gründungsgeschehens, Münster.

Porter, Michael E. (1990): The Competitive Advantage of Nations, New York.

Porter, Michael E. (1998): Cluster and the new Economics of Competition, in: Harvard Business Review, Vol. 76, No. 6, pp. 77-90.

Porter, Michael E. (2000a): Locations, Clusters and Company Strategy, in: Clark, Gordon L.; Feldman, Maryann P.; Gertler, Meric S. (eds.): The Oxford Handbook of Economic Geography, New York, pp. 253-275.

Porter, Michael E. (2000b): Location, Competition and Economic Development: Local Clusters in a Global Economy, in: Economic Development Quarterly, Vol 14, No. 1, pp. 15-34.

Porter, Michael (2002): Mehr Kunst als Wissenschaft, in McK Wissen, Vol. 1, pp. 20-25.

Prast, Franz (2008): Arbeitsmarktentwicklung in der Metropolregion Nürnberg, in: http://www.em-n.eu/fileadmin/mrn/Downloads/080418_Vortrag_Dr_Prast.pdf, accessed on May 19, 2010.

Raumordnungsbericht (2005), in: Bundesamt für Bauwesen und Raumordnung (eds.), Vol. 21, Bonn.

Regional-Monitor: Die Metropolregion Nürnberg – Zahlen.Karten.Fakten (2006), in: http://www.statistik.nuernberg.de/stat_inf/emn/2006/RM_EMN_2006.html, accessed on May 9, 2008.

Rosenfeld, Stuart A. (1997): Bringing Business Clusters into the Mainstream of Economic Development, in: European Planning Studies, Vol. 5, No. 1, pp. 3-23.

Russell, Daniel M.; Streitz, Norbert A.; Winograd, Terry (2005): Builing disappearing Computers, in: Communications of the ACM, Vol. 48, No. 3, pp. 42-48.

Sautter, Björn (2004): Regionale Cluster – Konzepte, Analyse und Strategie zur Wirtschaftsförderung, in: Standort – Zeitschrift für angewandte Geographie, Vol. 28, No. 2, pp. 66-72.

Schamp, Eike W. (2000): Vernetzte Produktion – Industriegeographie aus institutioneller Perspektive, Darmstadt.

Schiele, Holger (2003): Der Standortfaktor – Wie Unternehmen durch regionale Cluster ihre Produktivität und Innovationskraft steigern, Weinheim.

Schmiedl, Dieter; Niedermeyer, Georg (2006): Patentatlas Deutschland – Regionaldaten der Erfindungstätigkeit, München.

Scholz, Peter (2005): Softwareentwicklung eingebetteter Systeme – Grundlagen, Modellierung, Qualitätssicherung, Heidelberg.

Simon, David E. (1999): An embedded software primer, Boston.

Späth, Lothar (2003): Vorwort, in: Schiele, Holger: Der Standortfaktor – Wie Unternehmen durch regionale Cluster ihre Produktivität und Innovationskraft steigern, Weinheim, pp. 9-12.

Swann, Peter; Prevezer, Martha (1996): A comparison of the dynamics of industrial clustering in computing and biotechnology, in: Research Policy, Vol. 25, No. 7, pp. 1139-1157.

Turley, Jim (1999): Embedded processors by numbers, in: Embedded Systems Programming, Vol. 12, No. 5, pp. 13-14.

Van de Berg, Leo; Braun, Erik; van Winden, Willem (2001): Growth Clusters in European Cities: An Integral Approach, in: Urban Studies, Vol. 38, No. 1, pp. 185-205.

Weiterentwicklung raumordnungspolitischer Leitbilder und Handlungsstrategien, Beschluss der 32. Ministerkonferenz für Raumordnung am 28.04.2005 in Berlin.

Wirtschaftsbericht 2007 – Daten, Konzepte, Initiativen, in: http://www.wirtschaft. nuernberg.de/ver2004/decidedownloads/dl/Wirtschaftsbericht_2007_106.pdf, accessed on May 7, 2011.

Zeitlin, Jonathan (1992): Industrial districts and local economic regeneration - Overview and comment, in: Pyke, Frank; Sengenberger, Werner (eds.): Industrial Districts and Local Economic Regeneration. International Labour Organisation, Geneva, pp. 279-294.

MAIN FACTORS OF SUCCESS IN
MERGERS AND ACQUISITIONS' PERFORMANCE

STEFKA IANKOVA

(SOFIA UNIVERSITY "ST. KLIMENT OHRIDSKI", BULGARIA)

1. Introduction

Mergers and acquisitions (M&A) constitute strategic actions. The motivations of the protagonists are completely obvious: Through M&As the acquirers can gain immediate access to the technologies, distribution channels and market shares of the target companies. Acquisitions can bring capacities to acquiring companies that they consider inefficient to be developed internally. But even if these operations are increasing and are being undertaken with great enthusiasm by the executives, their post-merger effects may be quite controversial. This clear disparity between the popularity of M&As and their actual results is an interesting field to be investigated. Consequently, the objective of this article is to research the reasons behind this paradox and to establish a framework for a successful outcome of these deals.

The 1980s and 1990s were characterized with M&A waves that have transformed industries on the global scene and have affected the careers of millions of employees. In recent years this phenomenon continues to take place, especially in cross-border takeover transactions. However, when trying to assess their performances, it turns out that many of them did not succeed in attaining their initial goals.

Certainly, due to their utmost importance for the global economy, there have been significant discussions in the sphere of management, and some important considerations have been reached on the issue of how and over what periods of time M&A successes should be measured. Researchers in strategy (Lubatkin, 1993; Hambrick & Canella, 1993; Lieberman & Montgomery, 1988; Hayward, 2002 etc.) have tried to describe and to explain the main characteristics of this phenomenon. Despite their scientific efforts, acquisitions continued to appear as strategic maneuvers that in their essence are much more complex than initially assumed and new determinants of performance emerged over the years. For example, an acquiring company can make a wrong judgment when evaluating the target company, and, as a consequence, too high a premium price can be paid, or the post-merger integration process can be managed poorly. These factors appeared to be very useful if taken into consideration when making an attempt to explain why the M&As do not create enough value in terms of synergy and do not contribute to the increase in revenues of the acquiring companies. As an additional remark, the challenge of this article is to examine: What is the logic behind the fact that these transactions continue to be undertaken at an increasing rate if they do not really have a significant impact on the profitability of the acquiring companies?

In order to investigate these issues, in this article a synthesis of the main factors is proposed which are derived from the major works that have studied the M&A performance during the last decades. By the method of meta-analysis of research works in the field of M&A, ten main factors of success are identified. These factors are supported by the main theories in management and are their hypotheses are empirically proven in the discussed research papers.

Then these factors are empirically tested in the context of the Bulgarian M&A deals that occurred in the past 20 years. Through the means of factor analysis the essential factors are extracted and discussed. Some of the theoretical factors find strong support in this research, while others appear as completely irrelevant.

Lastly, the results of this study are reasoned in the institutional context of the country and its economic specificities. The reached conclusions on the successful M&A performances in Bulgaria can be interpreted and explained only partially by the theoretical concepts in the meta-analysis.

2. Literature review

If some of the results in this literature synthesis seem contradictory, this is due to the fact that in their analyses some researchers have focused narrowly on the financial and strategic variables as predictors of M&A performance, while others affirm that there is no clear relationship between these aspects because the human capital and the cultural fit are the predominant elements in the post-merger integration phase. For example, the most recent studies in this field deem organizational and cultural integration as critical success factors, and these studies are further complemented with very detailed models that explain the impact of managerial decisions and actions on the success of M&As. From here, different measurement techniques were employed and different results were obtained.

2.1 Portfolio diversification

Historically, the study of Lubatkin (1983) is the first profound research on mergers and acquisitions in the strategic management literature. The author measures the performance of the acquiring companies in M&A transactions. He is interested in investigating whether there is a real advantage for these companies from these operations. The basic theoretical idea is that mergers often constitute an act of diversification. This framework necessitates a strategic adjustment between the acquiring and the target company. This means: The more common characteristics the corresponding environments of the two companies have, the bigger the profit of the acquiring company will be.

This suggestion is based on the concept of synergy. Related to the strategic adjustment, synergy takes place when two separate entities can be managed more efficiently together than separately. This way they take advantage of lower costs or a better allocation of scarce resources in the present environmental constraints.

The first hypothesis formulated by Lubatkin is that M&As do not create competitive advantages. Further to this hypothesis, the author investigates the paradox why regardless of their obvious inefficiency, M&As continue to be performed. He gives two explications to this disparity: The first one is that the managers of the acquiring company make errors. Choosing the best target company and paying the just premium price on the deal is a complex process. For example, many elements must be taken into consideration, including risks and future cash flows. The second explication is that managers are motivated to maximize their personal wealth at the expense of the shareholders' well-being. Actually, the author claims that in big companies a conflict of interests can arise between the shareholders that own the company and the executives that manage it (Berle & Means, 1932). The salaries of these managers, their bonuses and other advantages are more related to the size of the company than to its profits. Thus, the prestige and the power are also directly related to the size of the company, rather than to its profit (Mueller, 1969). This gives explanation to the divergence between the apparently poor returns of M&As and their growing number.

The second hypothesis is that M&As create competitive advantage. This hypothesis can be effective but the advantages of M&As may not stand out in an obvious way. The reasons could be administrative problems that can emerge and lead to losing sight of the incurred advantages. In fact, it should be underlined that there are no indisputable methods for measuring the inefficiency. There is no objective measurement agreed upon as a yardstick for efficiency.

The main statement in this research is that the acquiring companies can benefit from M&As through technological and financial synergies, as well as from diversification. The ideas analyzed and supported in this research of Lubatkin (1983) lead to the conclusion that the significant gains from an M&A are incurred by the acquired company. A weakness in these ideas is that they consider M&As as a homogeneous phenomena. However, the strategic management literature reveals that an M&A does not constitute a homogeneous phenomenon. On the contrary, the results of such transactions seem to depend on the strategic adjustment between the acquiring and the target company.

2.2 Strategic similarity

Performance factors in the horizontal mergers were also described by Ramaswamy (1997). He investigates their impact in the banking industry. In his research work the author examines the influence of the strategic similarity between the acquiring and the target company on the post-merger performance. He suggests that mergers between banks with similar strategic characteristics reach higher performance indicators than mergers between banks lacking strategic similarity.

Previous studies have shown that a certain level of product-market proximity between the target and the acquiring company is a desirable characteristic in order to improve the post-M&A performance (Lubatkin, 1987; Singh & Montgomery, 1987). Other studies have shown that the compatibility in respect to technologies, organizational cultures, products and customer groups have an important influence on the performance (Chatterjee & Lubatkin, 1992). But few works have made an attempt to understand the differences in performance reached in the different types of M&As. The authors have come to the conclusion that, in general, related M&As outperform unrelated ones. In this respect, Ramaswamy (1997) extends this literature by focusing on horizontal mergers. He uses the concept of strategic similarity in order to explain the differences in performance that follow a banking merger.

His hypothesis that mergers between a target and an acquiring company with similar strategic characteristics outperform unrelated ones is fully supported in this research. The author investigated banking mergers that took place in a certain seven-year period (1984-90), taking into account a sample of 46 mergers (92 banks). He measured the performance with accounting measures of profitability. The results of the regression analysis allow supporting completely the hypothesis.

An interesting point in this respect is that even though the results are relevant, they contradict the results on the same research topic produced by Harrison (1991). In his multi-industrial study on M&As over a period of 20 years (1970-89) he finds that exactly the lack of similarities, rather than the existing similarities in R&D, assets, administrations, etc. is positively related to post-M&A performance. However, Harrison (1991) investigates simultaneously the related and the unrelated M&As, while Ramaswamy (1997) limits his work to horizontal mergers which means that he does not include vertical elements.

2.3 Characteristics of the executives

Kroll and Wright (1997) investigate the forms of control as a critical determinant of acquisition performance and CEO rewards. The authors argue that in the companies managed by external managers the M&As can be undertaken against the shareholders' interest because the remuneration of the executives is based on non-performance criteria. However, the remuneration of the managers in the companies that are managed by their owners is based on both, performance and non-performance criteria. The intrinsic idea of this research is that in the companies managed by their owners the stockholders can benefit from the M&As.

From the perspective of the principal agent theory in this study the authors analyze to what extent the M&As are launched in the interest of executives rather than in the interest of stockholders. The analysis is based on the measurement of the cumulative abnormal returns of the companies, taken as performance criteria. The growth in size or the revenues are accepted as non-performance factors. Meanwhile, Kroll and Wright (1997) juxtapose two research currents. The first one supports the idea that there is no relationship between the remuneration of the executives and their performance (Hambrick & Finkelstein, 1995). In fact, based on their empirical study, Jensen and Murphy (1990) conclude that the compensation of the executives is independent from their performance. The other research current supports the idea that the executives can strive to acquire companies acting in their own interest, rather than in the interest of the stockholders (Agrawal & Mandlker, 1987; Morck & al., 1990).

The authors prove empirically the hubris hypothesis according to which even if the executives acquire target companies that they assume that can be managed more efficiently by them, these M&As do not bring higher profitability (Hayward & Hambrick, 1997; Roll, 1986). The authors' results are in accordance with the portfolio theory that stipulates that the executives' goals are to diversify their personal welfare.

Seth, Song & Pettit (2002) also investigate the hubris hypothesis, as well as the hypothesis of managerialism, applied in the M&A context. Their results are concordant with the findings of Kroll and Wright (1997), i.e. that the executives make wrong judgments when taking a decision on an M&A transaction, motivated by non-performance criteria.

The most recent studies in this sphere pay attention to the leadership style of the top managers, involved in the M&A deal. Waldman and Javidan (2009) affirm that the post-M&A performance is strongly affected by the leadership factor. In their model they make a distinction between the "personalized charisma" of the executives that results in an absorption strategy and the "socialized charisma" of the executives that leads to collaborative vision-formation. The authors stipulate that the second type of leadership is more successful in the M&As.

2.4 Human capital

Cannella and Hambrick (1993) dedicate their research to the effects of the executive departures on the performance of acquired firms. In their hypothesis they argue that these departures are harmful to the post-M&A stage. According to their opinion, a higher status should be offered to the managers in the acquired company in order to preserve the conductive working environment. In their study the authors demonstrate to what extent the managers of the acquired company are an indispensable and fundamental element to the human resources of the target company and that their retention is an important determinant for the post-M&A performance.

Further to this study, Very, Lubatkin, Calori and Veiga (1997) base their research on the theory of relative standing. Their theory affirms that the own perception of the individual's status in the social framework emerges from their comparison to the others in the same social framework. The relational models in this theory refer to the theory of social comparison and the equity theory (Adam, 1965). Similar to Hambrick and Canella's (1993) approach, the authors analyze their hypotheses through the perspective of the perception of the acquired managers as the authors believe that what happens to the acquired managers affects the overall results in the organization.

In recent years the studies on the relationship between M&A performance and human resource practices continue to be a subject of thorough investigation. Weber and Tarba (2010) affirm that post-M&A integration can be improved through enhanced HR practices like training, communication and autonomy. The authors distinguish their model from the "resource based" view which has generally accepted that in order to produce a sustainable competitive advantage the acquirers must transfer those assets and people from the acquired firm that have different and better skills and knowledge than it and its competitors possess. On the contrary, Weber and Tarba (2010) propose a "knowledge based" view which emphasizes the necessity to develop and integrate knowledge. They are convinced that exploiting synergies by resource sharing is the winning strategy.

2.5 Cultural factors

One of the most popular factors in the M&A theory is the cultural difference between the participants. In its most general form, the hypothesis of cultural differences suggests that the difficulties, the costs and the risks associated with the cross-cultural contact increase with the increase of the cultural differences between two individual, groups or organizations (Hofstede, 1980). In accordance with that hypothesis, Stahl and Voigt (2004) develop this idea in terms of M&A integration. They prove that the cultures of the merging companies should be compatible in order to become successfully integrated. Respectively, the negative side of the cultural diversity is emphasized.

Calori, Lubatkin and Very (1994) also analyze the influence of the national culture and its relationship with the integration mechanisms in the international M&As. More precisely, they investigate the cross-border M&As through the perspective of the control mechanisms. They give evidence that the control mechanisms, being formal or informal, are related to the behavioral and economic performance of the acquired company. Their conclusion is that the acquiring companies should develop some kind of informal control and coordination, i.e. they should decrease the formal control on the operational decision-making level in order to improve the performance of their foreign acquisitions.

Child, Faulkner and Pitkethly (2002) develop the same idea in their research on the relationship between the level of integration and the degree of strategic and operational control in cross-border M&As. Their basic point is that to enhance the M&A performance, the acquiring companies should adopt an adaptive approach to their different international target companies. The authors are convinced that trying to implement a universal approach to different cultures is not a winning M&A strategy.

2.6 Acquired experience

The influence of the previous experience on the M&A performance has been widely discussed but the results are still controversial. Haleblian and Finkelstein (1999) conduct their research works on M&As from the perspective of the "learning theory". Their basic idea is that previous experience and M&A performance are related in a U-curve. However, the more the new target companies are similar to the previously acquired ones, the better the outcome of the transaction will be.

Later, Hayward (2002) provoked by this research, performed his own analysis on the topic and reached opposing results. For him, previous experience is a necessary but not a sufficient condition to assure the learning knowledge of the acquirer. His innovative idea is that the acquiring companies are influenced by a complexity of different kinds of experiences through which they develop specialized skills. In the same point of view, Beckman and Haunschild (2002) affirm that acquirers with previous heterogeneous acquisition experience have the tendency to pay lower premium prices for the additional M&As and this leads to a better performance.

Zollo and Singh (2004) extend their research in the knowledge-based view where the companies are regarded as sources of knowledge. The authors demonstrate that the codification of knowledge has a strong and positive influence on the M&A performance. The simple accumulation of experience has no influence. Finally, their point of view is that the level of integration between the two merging companies improves significantly the performance, while changes in the management team of the acquired company have a negative influence on the performance.

2.7 Early positioning

Carow, Heron and Saxton (2004) investigate questions on the M&A performance from the perspective of the participants' positioning in the M&A wave. They are convinced that the pioneer's situation can have a positive impact on the profit of the shareholders. The authors' idea is that companies that react earlier in the M&A wave have an advantage to their competitors because they can benefit from information asymmetry. This theory, discussed widely in the research of Lieberman and Montgomery (1988) as well as Barney (1988), has its application in the M&A theory because the researchers prove that the successful M&As are based on the early participants' actions to buy at a lower price an underestimated company and to create a unique combination of inimitable synergies.

2.8 Mode of financing

The decision on the mode of financing an M&A deal is a consequence of several considerations, like, for example, experience and the level of expertise. Hayward (2003) argues that there is a direct influence of the investment banks on the M&A decisions – starting from the selection of target companies to the method of payment of the transaction. He believes that by choosing more complex payment solutions the banks benefit from their expertise in order to influence the entire process of the transaction. They readily advise their corporate clients to finance their deals with a complex mix of financial instruments but the clients' interest is not always the priority in these deals. The author suggests that the less the acquiring companies turn to banks' expertise, and the less these companies finance their deals by stocks, the better their M&A performance will be.

This study was followed by another one on the same topic, performed by André, Kooli and L'Her (2004). These authors studied the relationship between post-M&A performance and the method of payment of the transaction. They prove that, in general, the M&A deals financed by stocks have a weaker performance in the long-run. In accordance with the idea of Loughran and Vijh (1997), they suggest that the acquirers should finance their M&As by means of stocks when their stocks are overestimated and by cash when their stocks are underestimated.

2.9 Synergy of resources

Capron and Pistre (2002) investigate the origin of the abnormal returns to the acquirers. Their basic idea is that there is a relationship between the acquirer's revenues and the resources of the target company or the acquirer. In other words, the researchers suggest that value realized by the acquirer results either from the target's or the acquirer's resources, or from both.

In their analysis the authors prove that the acquirers do not benefit from abnormal returns when they only receive resources from the target company. However, the acquirers can expect to benefit from abnormal returns when they transfer their own resources to the target company. Capron and Pistre (2002) affirm that the M&As create value for the acquirers when their competitors cannot reproduce the synergy and the financial capacities that result from this synergy. This is usually the case when the acquirer controls unique resources that can be used by the target company. Seth, Song and Pettit (2002) develop the same idea – that the M&As could be successful only when here is a sharing of the resources among the two participants.

Homburg and Bucerius (2005, 2006) also investigate the sources of synergy between the merging companies. They extend their studies on the post-M&A integration. The authors approach the integration process from the marketing perspective. The results of their analysis indicate that the marketing integration has a huge influence on the post-M&A performance, much more significant that the economies of scale on the industrial side. These results are concordant with the arguments, according to which there is a considerable risk of loosing customers following an M&A transaction.

During the integration phase the energy of the management is often concentrated on the organizational aspects of the deal, at the expense of the tasks related to the customers' satisfaction. Due to this, the quality of the customer service is likely to decrease. This situation creates incertitude in the clients' perceptions. As a consequence, the competitors may take advantage of this situation and can attract the hesitating customers. This point of view is completely in harmony with Morall's (1996) one – that the question on the clients' retention constitutes a central point for the success of M&As.

2.10 Governmental participation

Uhlenbruck and De Castro (2000) study the relationship between the privatization as an M&A transaction and the performance of the acquiring and the target company. According to the economic theory, the transfer of capital on the market and the market competition should improve the financial performance (Jensen, 1989). However, sometimes the empirical evidence contradicts this theory. Parker and Hartley (1991), for example, did not succeed in confirming the fact that the privatization improves the financial performance. Other researchers clearly suggest the contrary (Bishop, Kay & Mayer, 1994). In addition, some other studies approach the question from a different perspective. They investigate whether environmental conditions rather than ownership affect the performance more intensely.

The theory of M&As suggests that the performance of an M&A transaction is particularly influenced by the strategic and organizational adjustment between the merging companies, as well as by their integration and the process of transformation (Haspeslagh & Jemison, 1991; Sitkin, 1986; Lubatkin, 1983). Uhlenbruck and De Castro (2000) affirm that the adjustment and the process of transformation change radically when one of the parties in the transaction is the government. In fact, in the traditional framework of M&As, the seller is supposed to protect the interest of the stockholders only through the maximization of the selling price (Jemison & Sitkin, 1986) and, presumably, he is incapable of influencing the post-M&A process. But in the case of privatization, the government is the seller and its interests surpass the simple economic considerations. Consequently, the government can also impose its political or social considerations directly or indirectly even after the deal has taken place.

In this respect, the authors suggest that the strategic adjustment between the participating companies is important because the adjustment between the industrial know-how of the investors and the target companies' resources is a critical element of success.

2. Empirical analysis

The research task of this article is to verify whether the discussed Western theories and hypotheses regarding the M&A performance have their application in the Bulgarian business environment. Analogically to the theoretically deduced factors of success, a questionnaire was established, composed of 26 questions/variables. The answers to these questions are evaluated on a 5-point Likert scale. The database consists of 103 filled-in questionnaires that evaluate the performance of 103 M&A deals in Bulgaria. The questions were asked to managers who participated in these M&A transactions in Bulgaria. These managers were demanded to evaluate the M&A transaction of their company according to the 5-scale degree of relatedness (from "strongly agree" to "strongly disagree") to each question/variable.

This empirical model was analyzed through the factor analysis on SPSS. This multivariate statistical method of analysis is the most appropriate one in this case because the number of the initial variables is reduced while the greatest possible share of the common dispersion of the data is preserved (Manov, 2002).

3.1 Sampling adequacy

Sampling adequacy in factor analysis is measured in order to evaluate the correlation of the investigated variables. The adequacy in this statistical method is measured through Bartlett's Test of Sphericity and the Kaiser-Meyer-Olkin (KMO) coefficient. The results from the factor analysis of the initial database with 26 variables are shown in Table 1 below:

Table 1: Coefficients of sampling adequacy of the 26 variables

Kaiser-Meyer-Olkin Measure of Sampling Adequacy		.658
Bartlett's Test of Sphericity	Approx. Chi-Square	1130.594
	Degree of freedom	300
	Sig.	.000

The KMO coefficient of 0.658 is an appropriate value that gives reason to consider the initial sampling model as an adequate one. In the same time, the significance of the Bartlett's test is under the critical level of 0.05 what demonstrates that the null hypothesis for lack of correlation of the variables should be eliminated. However, in the analysis of the correlation matrix some other evidences can be found that should be taken in consideration.

3.2. Correlation matrix analysis

Some of the variables in the correlation matrix do not meet the fundamental condition, i.e. to be related strongly enough among themselves, but in a different degree. In general, as a practical rule, it is accepted that each variable should have at least one high in the absolute value coefficient of correlation with the rest of the variables. Nine of the variables do not meet this condition, and, respectively, could be eliminated from further analysis.

3.3. Extraction of factors

The factors are extracted through the Principal Components Method that is an extraction technique which reduces the number of variables while preserving as much information as possible on the initial variables, composing the specific matrix. Out of these 26 variables eight common factors are formed that have a dispersion of 74%. However, eight factors are difficult to be interpreted logically, especially when there are some vari-

ables that have very weak correlation coefficients with the other variables in the database, and that is why, in order to reach adequate and logical interpretation results, the factor analysis should proceed by eliminat-
ing the redundant variables.

2.4. Final results

When gradually all redundant variables for the M&A performance analysis are eliminated through the application of the above-mentioned
steps, a final sampling of nine variables that form three factors of successful M&A performance is reached. The results of the adequacy coefficients of these nine variables are demonstrated in Table 2.

Table 2: Coefficients of sampling adequacy of the 9 final variables

Kaiser-Meyer-Olkin Measure of Sampling Adequacy		.756
Bartlett's Test of Sphericity	Approx. Chi-Square	432.144
	Degree of freedom	36
	Sig.	.000

It is visible from the analysis of the above table that the KMO coefficient
and Bartlett's Test of Sphericity increase their values. That means that
the sampling with these nine final variables is even more adequate,
compared to the initial one with the 26 variable.

**Table 3: Results from the factor extraction –
common dispersion of the 9 final variables**

Compo-nent	Extraction Sums of Squared Loadings			Rotation Sums of Squared Loadings		
	Total	Percent-age of variance	Cumulative percentages	Total	Percent-age of variance	Cumulative percentages
1	4.104	45.595	45.595	2.572	28.580	28.580
2	1.618	17.983	63.578	2.252	25.028	53.607
3	1.183	13.149	76.727	2.081	23.120	76.727

In Table 3 where the results from the common factors extraction are
demonstrated, we find that these nine variables form three common factors with a dispersion of 76.72%. These results give us the foundation for
a logical interpretation of the main factors in the M&A performance. Interpretation of the results is done on the basis of the rotated component
matrix; see Table 4, where the variables are grouped, according to their
correlation, in three common factors.

Table 4: Rotated component matrix of the 9 final variables

	Component		
	1	**2**	**3**
v2 market share increase	**.889**	.172	.078
v7 same industry	**.892**	.097	.186
v17 previous M&A experience	**.825**	.110	.119
v9 employees resistance	-.020	.149	**.911**
v10 IT integration	.313	.084	**.797**
v12 strategic adjustment	.203	**.707**	.446
v14 brand name recognition	.229	**.719**	.211
v15 new products development	-.039	**.879**	-.105
v11 common corporate culture	.333	**.619**	.554

From the analysis of this matrix the following three common factors for a successful M&A performance of the Bulgarian companies are identified:

Factor I: Industry relatedness;

Factor II: Common marketing strategy and corporate culture convergence;

Factor III: Managed employees' resistance and integrated technological processes.

The first factor in the successful M&A deals in Bulgaria comprises the variables that characterize the industry relatedness between the merging companies:

- the goal of the M&A was to eliminate a competitor and to increase the own market share (variable 2);
- the deal was between companies operating in the same industry (variable 7);
- the acquiring company had an extensive previous experience in M&As in the same industry (variable 17).

From here it can be inferred that the M&As in Bulgaria among direct competitors are the most successful ones. Previous M&A experiences in the same industry have a positive influence on the outcome of the transaction.

The second factor combines the following four variables:

In the M&A transaction the following processes were challenged:

- the creation of a common corporate culture among the merging companies (variable 11);
- strategic adjustments (variable 12);
- imposing brand name recognition on the market (variable 14);

- the development of new products (variable 15).

These variables refer to the challenges in the M&A process and can be related to the marketing approach by means of a common marketing strategy and corporate cultural convergence of the participants. This factor gives a clear idea that, in order to maximize the results of an M&A in Bulgaria, the efforts of the merging companies should be strategically directed to combining the commercial approach and the creation of a common corporate image of the new entity. This factor is particularly important for the marketing and PR departments in the organization for in the post-M&A stage it should pay attention to the strategic adjustment of maintaining the existing customers and attracting new ones.

The third factor is entirely related to the internal organizational and operating activities of the companies. It combines two variables that characterize the human capital and the technological state of the companies: In these respects, by an M&A transaction the following processes were challenged:

- employees' resistance (variable 9);
- IT integration (variable 10).

The importance of this third factor for the HR departments and the technical management is pivotal for the merging companies in Bulgaria. It can be inferred from its interpretation that for the success of an M&A, considerable attention should be paid to the employees who in this process will resist the new situation and the uncertainty. The key solution for a successful integration of the teams is this: The employees have to be trained in the new IT systems and technologies so that the operating processes will not be hampered.

The results from this factor analysis for the Bulgarian M&A transactions find support in the literature reviews on this subject. They are in accordance with Lubatkin's (1998) theory of diversification, Hayward's (2003) views on the accumulated experience in related industries, Homburg and Burcerius's (2005) findings on synergy through marketing integration, and Weber's (2010) affirmations on the relationship between M&A performance and management's focus on human capital of the merging companies.

Variables that measure the characteristics of the executives (Canella & Hambrick, 1993), the control mechanisms (Child, Faulkner & Pitkethly, 2002) and the cultural differences of the merging companies (Stahl & Voigt, 2004) are eliminated from the factor analysis due to their weak correlation coefficients. The explanation of these results can be found in the fact that the investigated participants in this research are big international companies that acquired Bulgarian companies. Consequently, the global vision of management in these M&As is also an international one, successfully imposed by the acquirers. The conclusion that can be drawn on the basis of this study is that the empirical research lacks the specificity of the institutional context for the country, but implies mostly the international perspective on M&As.

3. Conclusion

By the analysis of existing literature, ten major performance factors of M&As could be identified in the strategic management theories. The empirical factor analysis for the Bulgarian M&A deals that took place in the last 20 years gave support to the hypothesis of similarity, largely discussed in the M&A theory. Similarity, being the most important factor for successful M&A performance, can be interpreted on several levels.

First, similarity can be analyzed in terms of portfolio diversification. In the context of this research, M&A deals in Bulgaria between companies with similar activities have a higher probability to succeed. Second, the similarity can be investigated on a strategic level. The probability for a successful performance increases when the merging companies have identical strategic goals. Third, the inner organizational similarity is a favorable performance factor.

Some limiting aspects in this study imply an interest in a further and more profound analysis of empirical facts. For example, its sample comprises 103 cases of M&As in Bulgaria. That is a relatively limited size and could be developed. Also, opinions of top and middle managers were taken into consideration being subjective elements for an evaluation of a successful M&A performance.

However, this paper proposes ideas for future research and gives a perspective on the performance factors that could be further adapted and developed in relation to the processes of privatization or the post-merger integration. Specifically, a separate research can be developed on the subject of M&As in the Bulgarian banking sector which has a strong influence on the economic climate of the country. Also, the extracted factors could be tested and applied in a broader setting of Eastern European M&As that took place during the same 20-years period.

References

Adam J. (1965), 'Inequity in social exchange'. Academic Press, New York, pp. 267-299.

Agrawal A. & Mandelker G. (1987), 'Managerial incentives and corporate investment and financing decisions'. *Journal of Finance*, 42, pp. 823-837.

André P., Kooli M. & L'Her J. (2004), 'The long-run performance of mergers and acquisitions: evidence from the Canadian stock market', *Financial Management*, Winter 2004, pp. 27-43.

Barney, J (1988). 'Returns to bidding firms in mergers and acquisitions: Reconsidering the relatedness hypothesis', *Strategic Management Journal*, 9, pp. 71-78.

Beckman C. & Haunschild P. (2002), 'Network learning: the effects of partners' heterogeneity of experience on corporate acquisitions', *Administrative Science Quarterly*, 47, pp. 92-124.

Berle A. & Means G. (1932), 'The modern corporation and private property'. New York: Macmillan Company.

Calori R., Lubatkin M. & Very P. (1994), 'Control mechanisms in cross-border acquisitions: an international comparison', *Organisation studies*, 15/3, pp. 361-379.

Calori R., Lubatkin M., Very P. & Veiga J. (1997), 'Relative standing and the performance of recently acquired European firms', *Strategic Management Journal*, 18:8, pp. 593-614.

Cannella A. & Hambirck D. (1993), 'Effects of executive departures on the performance of acquired firms', *Strategic Management Journal*, 14, pp. 137-152.

Capron L. & Pistre N. (2002), 'When do acquirers earn abnormal returns ?', *Strategic Management Journal*, 23, pp. 781-794.

Carow K., Heron R. & Saxton T.(2004), 'Do early birds get the returns? An empirical investigation of early-mover advantages in acquisitions', *Strategic Management Journal*, 25, pp.563-585.

Chaterjee S. & Lubatkin M. (1990), 'Corporate mergers, stockholder diversification, and changes in systematic risk', *Strategic Management Journal*, 11, pp. 255-268.

Child J., Faulkner D. & Pitkethly R. (2002), 'The management of international acquisitions' *Academy of Management Review*, Jan. 2002. pp. 129-132.

Haleblian J. & Finkelstein S. (1999), 'The influence of organizational acquisition experience on acquisition performance: A behavioral learning perspective', *Administrative Science Quarterly*, 44, pp. 29-56.

Hambrick D. & Cannella A. (1993), 'Relative standing : A framework for understanding departures of acquired executives', *Academy of Management Journal*, 36 :4, pp. 733-762.

Hambrick D. & Finkelstein (1995), 'The effects of ownership structure on conditions on conditions at the top: The case of CEO pay rises', *Strategic Management Journal*, 16:3, pp. 175-193.

Harrison J., Hitt M. & Hoskisson R. (1991), 'Synergies and post-acquisition performance : differences versus similarities in resource allocation', *Journal of Management*, 17, pp. 173-190.

Haspeslagh P. & Jemison D. (1991), 'Managing acquisitions: creating value through corporate renewal', New York: The Free Press.

Hayward M. & Hambrick D. (1997), 'Explaining the premiums paid for large acquisitions: evidence of CEO hubris'. *Administrative Science Quarterly*, 42, pp. 103-127.

Hayward M. (2002), 'When do firms learn from their acquisition experience? Evidence from 1990-1995', *Strategic Management Journal*, 23, pp. 21-39.

Hayward M. (2003), 'Professional influence: the effects of investment banks on clients' acquisition financing and performance', *Strategic Management Journal*, 24, pp. 783-801.

Hofstede (1980), 'Culture's consequences: International differences in work-related values'. Sage, London.

Homburg C. & Bucerius M. (2005), 'A marketing perspective on mergers and acquisitions: How marketing integration affects postmerger performance', *Journal of Marketing*, 69, pp.95-113.

Homburg C. & Bucerius M. (2006), 'Is speed of integration really a success factor of mergers and acquisitions? An analysis of the role of internal and external relatedness', *Strategic Management Journal*, 27, pp. 347-367.

Jemison D. & Sitkin S. (1986), 'Corporate acquisitions: A process perspective', *Academy of Management Review*, 11, pp. 5-50.

Jensen M. et Murphy K. (1990), 'Performance pay and top management incentives', *Journal of Political Economy*, 98, pp. 225-264.

Lieberman M. & Montgomery D. (1988), 'First-mover advantages', *Strategic Management Journal*, 9, pp. 41-58.

Loughran T. & Vijh A. (1997), 'Do long-term shareholders benefit from corporate acquisitions ?', *Journal of Finance*, 52, pp. 1765-1790.

Lubatkin M. (1983), 'Mergers and the performance of the acquiring firm', *Academy of Management Review*, 8:2, pp. 218-225.

Lubatkin M. (1987), 'Merger strategies and stockholder value', *Strategic Management Journal*, 8:1, pp. 39-53.

Morall K. (1996), 'Managing a merger without losing customers', *Bank Marketing*, 28:3, pp. 18–23.

Manov A (2002), 'Multivariate statistical methods with SPSS', UNSS, Sofia, pp. 173-200.

Morck R., Shleifer A., & Vishny R. (1990), 'Do managerial objectives drive bad acquisitions?'. *Journal of Finance*, 25, pp. 31-48.

Mueller D. (1969), 'A theory of conglomerate mergers'. *Quarterly Journal of Economics*, 83, pp. 644-660.

Ramaswamy K. (1997), 'The performance impact of strategic similarity in horizontal mergers: Evidence from the US banking industry', *Academy of Management Journal*, 40:3, pp. 697-715.

Roll R. (1986), 'The hubris hypothesis of corporate takeovers'. *Journal of Business*, 59, pp. 197-216.

Seth. A., Song. K. & Pettit R. (2002), 'Value creation and destruction in cross-border acquisitions : an empirical analysis of foreign acquisitions of US firms', *Strategic Management Journal*, 23, pp. 921-940.

Singh H. & Montgomery C. (1987), "Corporate acquisition strategies and economic performance," *Strategic Management Journal*, 8 :4, pp. 377–86.

Stahl G. & Voigt A. (2004), 'Meta-analyses of the performance implications of cultural differences in mergers and acquisitions', *Academy of Management Best Conference Paper 2004* IM:I1.

Uhlenbruck K. & De Castro J. (2000), 'Foreign acquisitions in Central and Eastern Europe: Outcomes of privatization in transitional economies', *Academy of Management Journal*, 43:3, pp. 381-402.

Waldman D. & Javidan M. (2009), 'Alternative forms of charismatic leadership in the integration of mergers and a acquisitions', *The Leadership Quarterly*, 20 (2009), pp. 130-142.

Weber Y. & Tarba S. (2010), 'Human resources practices and performance of mergers and acquisitions in Israel', *Human Resource Management Review*, 20 (2010), pp. 203-211.

Wright P., Kroll M., Toombs L. & Leavell H. (1997), 'Form of control: a critical determinant of acquisition performance and CEO rewards', *Strategic Management Journal*, 18:2, pp. 85-96.

Zollo M. & Singh H. (2004), 'Deliberate learning in corporate acquisitions: Post-acquisition strategies and integration capability in US bank mergers', *Strategic Management Journal*, 25, pp. 1233-1256.

CHAPTER THREE:

SUSTAINABLE DEVELOPMENT IN THEORY AND APPLICATION

SUSTAINABILITY: WHY THE HONOURABLE MERCHANT WINS IN THE END

JOACHIM SCHWALBACH

(HUMBOLDT-UNIVERSITY, BERLIN, GERMANY)

Disregarding *"The General Principle of the Honourable Merchant"* (GPHM) is one of the major reasons for the recent financial crisis. In this context, for example, one may well call the investment adviser and former non-executive chairman of the NASDAQ stock market, Bernhard L. Madoff, a prototype of a dishonourable merchant ("It's all a big lie"). However, one must concede that his misconduct has only become possible through lax control by the auditors and the supervisory authorities as well as through the greed of the small and big investors for higher returns irrespective of the risks. Although the reasons for the financial crisis are manifold, the misconduct of the actors has primarily something to do with their individual nature rather than the institutions. In this respect, returning to the GPHM seems to be imperative.

The GPHM defines criteria of character and culture. Their compliance acts as harmoniser for the acting of entrepreneurs and society. You can trace this concept back to medieval Italy. As early as 1340, Italian merchants' books talk about the "true and honest merchant". In Germany, the rise of the *Hanse* is inseparably linked with the image of the Honourable Merchant. The loose league of towns that was the *Hanse* could only achieve the magnitude that determined history through mutual tolerance and virtuous behaviour of its members. In this sense, the GPHM describes a life philosophy whose realisation lets businessmen become mature, responsible and above all economically successful personalities. For the Honourable Merchant, business success and moral are no diverging interests. On the contrary: moral defined as sense of responsibility is considered a prerequisite for economic success that is not only seen as self-interest but also as a means to create sustainable values.

In the financial crisis we can distinguish between two dimensions of respectability: the respectability of the protagonists in day-to-day business and taking on corporate responsibility.

1. The *meaning of honour in the day-to-day business* in the form of confidence in the business partner is made impressively clear during the financial crisis by the incapacitation of the banks as a result of the misconduct of individual financial managers. The loss of trust that was a result of the disregard of the virtue of honesty lead to a loss in business and ultimately the big, global business network came to a stop. The leap of

faith necessary in a global financial market with high transaction speed did no longer exist. Transactions between banks did no longer take place. Without the co-ordinated intervention of the governments that was meant to renew the trust in the market, the system most likely would have ground to a halt – with catastrophic effects on both the global economy and the global society. In a world, in which also financial managers follow the GPHM, the situation would hardly have escalated to such an extent.

2. The second dimension of the GPHM refers to the *societal responsibility of the financial economy*. The honourable financial manager has to counteract the short-term pressure to yield high returns with a sound character and to defend his corporate and social responsibility against financial gamblers and soldiers of fortune. Without governmental intervention, existing internal control mechanisms seem to work only inadequately. In so far, global institutions are necessary and desirable to control compliance with honesty in the course of business and to sanction breaches. However, they can never completely replace the individual responsibility of Honourable Merchants.

The financial crisis reveals both societal and intra-corporate deficits in the basic understanding of responsible, sustainable and honourable and thus successful management. Hence, the GPHM is of utmost importance now and in the future. It should make entrepreneurs and managers aware that responsible behaviour is the basis of sustainable economic success and of social peace in the society. Concentrating on one's own historical roots and the present situation, may lead to a contemporary awareness of honesty among entrepreneurs and managers that expresses a cultural capability of development. A modern Honourable Merchant has a pronounced sense of responsibility on both the enterprise and the societal level. This includes fair behaviour towards employees, customers and business partners whom he continues to treat according to virtuous principles aiming to establish and to keep long-term relations. Social responsibility expresses itself through decisions taking into account stakeholders' interest, engagement at the company location, informing the public and politics, defending the social market economy and paying regard to environmental protection in all decisions made.

The GPHM is mostly related to owner-managed and family-owned enterprises, in short: to small and medium-sized businesses. However, it is precisely the medium-sized businesses who still fail to communicate their principles of a responsible management to a sufficient degree, thereby supporting the widespread public opinion that all businesswomen and businessmen behave erratically, whereas in fact only a few managers do. On the contrary: to stabilize the trust in the efficiency of a social market economy, it is necessary that in particular the small and medium-sized businesses inform about their contribution to the economy and the society.

In addition, the financial crisis should initiate a corporative discourse on the relationship between society and economy. Should this discourse not take place, there might be the risk that those prevail who in principle query the model of a social market economy. Starting point of the discourse should be the maxim that economy and society are mutually dependent. On the one hand, enterprises can primarily prosper in modern societies that are characterised by a high educational background, functioning markets and distinct legal certainty. On the other hand, modern societies depend on successful enterprises, because only they can increase the wealth of the society through market success. Thus enterprises and society are mutually dependent. This also means that activities of the one side are hardly successful if they are carried out at the expense of the other side.

The targeted discourse between economy, science, politics and civil society, however, should not predominantly concentrate on the abstract enterprise level but rather on the individual level of entrepreneur and manager and the bodies controlling them. It is precisely on the individual level that we have the chance to approach the subject of corporate social responsibility comprehensibly via the GPHM. In this context it can be proved that the vast majority of our executives act responsibly and that ultimately the Honourable Merchant in the sense of sustainability and responsibility is the winner for the enterprise and for society.

References

For further information on the subject of the Sustainability and the Honorable Merchant see:
www.der-ehrbare-kaufmann.de
www.csr-hu-berlin.org

SOCIAL AND ECONOMIC STRATEGIES FOR A SUSTAINABLE SOCIETY

DIETER FLÄMIG

(BERLIN, GERMANY)

1. European responsibility in times of globalization

The question of developing a sustainable and viable society demands a deep examination of the roots, potentials and risks of our present day societies and economies. Within the context of globalization these are constantly forced to align their reasoning and acting stronger with the constraints of international economic competition.

In his book "Globalization and its discontents" Joseph Stiglitz, Nobel Prize winner in Economics, sees the danger of a world-wide, at some point uncontrollable destabilization, which will have an effect on all important areas of life within our modern civilizations:

„Unfortunately, so far, those responsible for managing globalization, while praising these positive benefits, all too often have shown an insufficient appreciation of this adverse side, the threat to cultural identity and values ... If globalization continues to be conducted in the way that it has been in the past, if we continue to fail to learn from our mistakes, globalization will not only succeed in promoting development but will continue to create poverty and instability" (Stiglitz 2002: 247-248).

He wrote this in 2002, thus well before the culmination of the last major financial crisis and before the urgent appeal from the Intergovernmental Panel on Climate Change of 2007 to significantly curb global warming through world-wide efforts (see IPCC 2007: 4. Progress Report).

Stiglitz opts for a world-wide "multipronged strategy of reform" (Stiglitz 2002: 251), in order to put "a human face" (Stiglitz 2002: 252) on globalization. However, especially since 2007/2008 the financial crisis and its current consequences have demonstrated dramatically that our present global society is increasingly leading into perilous instability, which continuously distracts political concentration from systematic changes in the course towards a more stable and sustainable future to the numerous pressing rescue tasks.

Yet, in these times marked by ambivalences and dangers, Europe must, already in its own interest, assume a leading responsibility, not only as a political promoter of global reform processes, but also as an intelligent source of stimulus for an ecologically, socially and culturally exemplary society through its own acts in real life practice. The spiritual Europe is the intellectual home of the industrial revolution as well as the theoretical and political examination of its stages and consequences; it is hence predestined.

Such an understanding of self-responsibility is a great chance to revive Europe's best cultural values through exemplary action – in the European countries and anywhere in world, where our help for sustainable developments is needed.

2. The role of the public sphere

The ubiquitously apparent social transformation will be more extensive than those changes often associated with the years 1789 and 1989.

In his book *"The Culture of Power and the Power of Culture"*, which is substantially based on Jürgen Habermas's *habilitation* thesis *"Strukturwandel der Öffentlichkeit"*[1], T.C.W. Blanning deals with the social changes before the French Revolution. In 1962 Habermas had developed the idea of a *"öffentlicher Raum"* (public sphere), which is also applicable to current social demands. This "public sphere"-definition describes the phenomenon that, through communication in a society, content is actively being conveyed thus creating a "public sphere" which has an own authority and derives its cohesiveness from within itself (Blanning 2002: 5-14).

Blanning sums up very clearly: "Two interconnected developments had dissolved the old order: the exchange of goods and the exchange of information. Together they created a fundamentally different kind of public sphere – the bourgeois ..." (Blanning 2002: 8), which means the civil "public sphere" (see Blanning 2006: 19). This civil "public sphere" generated a social dynamic, which mostly led to the changes in Europe we have experienced and still experience today. It can also be the key to a future of sustainability, if today's civil society brings up the will, the knowledge and the strength for this purpose.

3. The global change requires ethical foundations

Globalization has led to a new quality with respect to the capitalistic exchange of goods; the era of internet, a sort of twin of globalization, has accelerated, multiplied and spread the exchange of information to a revolutionary degree.

The "public sphere", which Habermas already saw endangered e.g. through the manipulation of the consumer (see Blanning 2002: 11), is now faced with a difficult test under conditions by which its own increasing dynamic results into almost incomprehensible developments.

---

[1] "The structural transformation of the public sphere".

The erosion of the long-established system of values through the change of circumstances, also noted by Stiglitz, is followed by a universality in thinking and acting, marked by fears, trends and an instinct driven mindset. This is tragic, considering that especially now, in times of global complexity, when an inner compass is needed more than ever, it seems that its substance is dissolving.

The German psychologist Horst-Eberhard Richter sums up the problem as followed:

„Heute droht kein Hitler mehr. Aber was sich wieder einschleicht, ist neuer moralischer Verfall: eine egoistische Brutalisierung, von der atomaren Bedrohung angefangen bis zur Naturzerstörung und zu dem noch immer ungebremsten Zocker-Unwesen in der Finanzbranche...Die Barbarei liegt in einer moralischen Fühllosigkeit, einem Schwinden von Sensibilität"[2] (Richter 2002: 19).

In this context, already in 1978 the philosopher Carl-Friedrich von Weizsäcker called for an *"Ethos für die technische Welt"*[3] (C. Weizsäcker 1978: 90). He points out, that e.g. at first also the beginnings of the agricultural cultivation of land led to the destruction of nature and only later landscape care slowly became popular within the framework of learning processes, which are also applicable today. His postulate for our future is: We once again need more the *"Tugenden der Bescheidenheit und der Selbstbeherrschung"*[4] (C. Weizsäcker 1978: 91).

Those are ethical goals, which are easy to comprehend, but are they not only secondary virtues, which require an ontological foundation? The great religions could present support in this respect. However, despite numerous international efforts e.g. towards ecumenical similarities, unfortunately up to now there seems to be no evidence that those or related initiatives brought forth a sustainable world ethic for all people. In fact, vested rights probably not only exist in a material sense but also in terms of religion ...

In search of a common humanism, which includes the preservation of life and respectively of nature, human dignity and social responsibility, we sadly all to often encounter social-political pragmatism in the economized sphere, which allows power interests, short-sighted egoism and

---

[2] Today Hitler is no longer a threat. But what creeps in again, is a new moral decay: a selfish brutalization, starting from the atomic threat going up to the destruction of nature and the still unbroken presence of the nuisance of gamblers in the financial sector ...The barbarism originates from moral lack of feeling, a disappearance of sensibility.

[3] Ethos for the technical world.

[4] Virtues of modesty and self-control.

inhumane instincts. It has to be clarified, whether perhaps the former civil values bear joint responsibility for this set of problems seemingly inherent in the system.

In the course of this, John Gray from London School of Economics advises us to radically break with the destructive occidental humanistic idea of a legitimate claim to infinite socio-cultural and economic progress. He refers to Lao Tse and outs us humans as "straw dogs", who finally need to learn that this earth was not exclusively created for them, but rather that is makes up our home only for so long as we, by our behaviour, permit it to be (see Gray 2002).

Especially in Europe this requires a consequent discussion-based rethinking, that has to consequentially overcome those nearly medieval mindsets that continue to have an effect on us and regard humans as centre of universal being. In spite of all pressures to act: when climate and structural changes might occur, in the long run we will not be able to create a sustainability-oriented community of responsibility without a world-wide intellectual process of self-discovery.

4. Clarity with respect to the quality of changes

In this regard the German sociologist Meinhard Miegel puts forward helpful indications, which are of general validity:

- *„Zum ersten Mal in der Menschheitsgeschichte geht es um wirkliche Existenzfragen"*[5] (Miegel 2011: 95). *"Denn wie die westliche Wirtschafts- und Lebensweise Umwelt und Natur existenziell gefährdet, gefährdet sie auch die Stabilität des gesellschaftlichen Gefüges"*[6] (Miegel 2011: 134).
- *„Eine vernunftgesteuerte Debatte ist schwierig. Die Gesellschaft schützt nämlich ihr Eigenverständnis, das sie über Generationen hinweg entwickelt hat, durch Tabus"*[7] (Miegel 2011: 135). – He also refers to the taboos related to progress and improvement, which are closely linked to the values of traditional humanism. John Gray described this phenomenon as the cause and origin for today's overstraining of persons and societies.
- *"Die menschheitsgeschichtlich beispiellose Wachstumsorgie der zurückliegenden Jahrzehnte hat die Völker der frühindustrialisierten Länder in ei-*

---

[5] For the first time in the history of mankind questions of existence are truly at stake…

[6] For in the same way that the western economic and general way of life existentially harms the environment and nature, it also harms the stability of the social structure as such.

[7] A rational debate is difficult. Society uses taboos to protect its self-perception, a concept that has been developed over decades.

nen Rauschzustand versetzt, in dem sie möglichst verharren möchten"[8]
(Miegel 2011:163).
After nearly four billion years of biological evolution and about 30,000 years of intensive cultural development we, the people, suddenly painfully experience that our progress-oriented, ethically well justifiable way of thinking, acquired over generations, tested and accommodated to our needs, in reality more and more collides with the natural living condition. It goes without saying that the number of losers in this fatigue process which already seems to be irreversible constantly rises and that the losers are likely to lay the blame on those who lead them.

This is indicated for one thing by the revolutions in the baby boomer Arabic countries, which suffer from scarce resources, the lack of jobs and plutocratic restrictions, as well as the current youth revolts in European countries. However, this pressure can only bring about changes, if it leads to social conditions, which move the permanent interactions among people, their self-reflection and their learning processes away from obsolete vulgar-materialistic progress-oriented mindsets, which misunderstand our planet as inexhaustible self-service outlet of mankind.

If we really want existence ensuring social changes, we must get involved open-minded and free of traditional and modern prejudices. We need to change ourselves.

5. Making use of our best basics and values and ensuring the new perspective through concrete long-term consensus efforts

The European societies must not now make the mistake to entirely question their humanistic foundations and the social and economic systems based thereon. For the preservation of the creation and the maintenance of life are values, which in fact will remain as important as the idea of responsibility in liberty. In practice, these values constitute keys for a necessary shift in thinking, which now needs to be initialised within the frame of an intense social discussion and on the basis of a lasting consensus between the elites and the other involved stakeholders. Only in this way it is possible to pick up society, the majority of citizens, consumers and producers, in this most decisive 21st century.

A target-oriented comprehensive social discussion can generate its own quality of ethic and moral agreements, a self-commitment by the people with far-reaching consequences beyond generations, in order to

---

[8] The unprecedented growth orgy in the history of human race during the last decades has led the people of only early industrialised states into a state of intoxication, in which they are eager to remain.

reconcile society with nature and to declare exactly this goal to the enduring central social norm, as the centre of a new social contract. This is a norm with a high degree of relevance – ontologically and existentially barely surpassable –which ought to and will have consequences, due to its topicality, on governance, jurisdiction, education, upbringing, economic activity, income, personal behaviour etc.

In Germany this succeeded tendentially but still rudimentarily e.g. with the turning to alternative energy sources, which combines a withdrawal from the problematic nuclear energy with an ambitious general steering towards renewable energies (goal: 80-90% energy production from renewable energies until 2050). Yet this can only mark the beginning (see the reports on the German *"Erneuerbare-Energien-Gesetz 2011"*)[9].

In contrast to thinkers like Carl Amery, who in 1976 demanded the destruction of the industrial system (Amery 1976: 184), considering 7 bn. people, increasing world-wide poverty and having to face a mountain of tasks in terms of sustainability, now we must attempt an ecologically consequent reorganisation of the industrial and commercial systems yet avoiding economic deadlock and chaos.

We must turn the force of change of this further developed exchange of goods into a socially accepted and promoted "green" force, a worldwide long-term "green" cycle of development.

6. For a critical realism in the pursuit of sustainability and its media context

The "public sphere", meaning the exchange of information as basis for an influential, formative public, will, especially in the phases until a society of sustainability has reached its completion, be of utter importance.

This "public sphere" has gone through significant changes compared to the time of 1789 due to the technological possibilities on offer in this ruling era of information. The rapid availability of information, the acceleration of communication processes, the dynamic world of journalistic media, the diversity and vitality of sources, the multitude of information channels, the active participation of many millions of individual actors etc., which this new age of information and communication technology has brought to us, is like a big magic workshop with an impact potential we can hardly overlook from this point. However, we do realize that we are being massively influenced on a daily basis.

Thus, in the virtual world of communication just as in the traditional world it is ultimately decisive, who becomes best at mastering the "agenda setting", the ability to foreground issues, to set priorities with

---

[9] Law on renewable energies.

regard to contents. This is also one of the determining factors for the formation of sustainability-oriented majorities within a society. In this context, however, the problem arises that on the account of an unclear understanding of the validity and usability of the diverse information many target persons may and will respond with indetermination and inertia with respect to system-surmountable efforts.

Before the internet-revolution Neil Postman in his famous book *"Amusing Ourselves to Death"* already emphasized: In a culture or society the available communication media have a dominant influence on the orientation of the intellectual and social ambitions[10]. Postman, who among other things addressed the problem of an overarching infotainment, warned against incapacitation of the individual at the sight of mighty medial mainstreams. In the German publication of his book he stressed:

> *"Wie die Sprache selbst, so begründet auch jedes neue Medium einen bestimmten, unverwechselbaren Diskurs, indem es dem Denken, den individuellen Ausdruck, dem Empfindungsvermögen eine neue Form zur Verfügung stellt"*[11] (Postman 1985: 19).

The engaged, critical civil society as elixir of life of a free democratic society that should arouse its powers of self-renewal from within its midst for a sustainable society, is yet in danger, if its citizens allow no other than the for the most part solely by self-interest driven actors standing behind the predominant media to think and sense in their stead. People on all levels of responsibility, who only orientate themselves towards trends and published public opinions, won't in case of doubt bring up the necessary moral courage and individual mental work to undertake the difficult path to a society of sustainability. This path is highly probable to make it necessary to overcome cherished cognitive possessions, which have been backed and celebrated by medially created and respectively nurtured populism for centuries.

7. The responsible citizen must control and limit the role of computers

In his book *"Pay back"* Frank Schirrmacher brings up even closer today's communicative challenge.

---

[10] In the German version: *"..., daß die in einer Kultur verfügbaren Kommunikationsmedien einen beherrschenden Einflug auf die Orientierung der intellektuellen und sozialen Bestrebungen innerhalb dieser Gesellschaft haben"* (Postman 1985: 19).

[11] Just like language itself creates its particular, distinctive discourse, so does each medium, through providing a new form to one's thinking, individual expression, aesthesia.

„Wir scheinen zu glauben, dass wir unsere Intelligenz, Bildung und Kreativität dadurch sichern, dass wir mit den Computern in einer Art spannungsgeladener Koexistenz leben. Aber es gibt keine Koexistenz. Wir müssen die Computer tun lassen, was sie tun können, damit wir frei werden, ..., um sie mit neuen Befehlen zu versorgen"[12] (Schirrmacher 2009: 214). This freedom, however, is less a question of the individual time budget, but rather, above all, one of the free will, Schirrmacher concludes (see Schirrmacher 2009: 221).

Yet this free will, this freedom is a central ally of the social striving for sustainability: *"Vielleicht ist der freie Wille eine Illusion, und die Computermodelle, die ihn widerlegen, haben Recht. Aber es ist eine Illusion, die ... der Gesellschaft nützt, weil sie ihr das Fortbestehen ermöglicht"*[13] (Schirrmacher 2009: 221-222).

Schirrmacher especially addresses schools and colleges which should again lay a stronger emphasis on teaching independent thinking and the "value of the right question". His central conclusion: *"Es geht um Realitäten. In Schulen, Universitäten und an den Arbeitsplätzen muss das Verhältnis zwischen Herr und Knecht, zwischen Mensch und Maschine neu bestimmt werden"*[14] (Schirrmacher 2009: 224).

If we want to reach a society of sustainability, we need to understand this responsible thinking, at most without manipulation, starting from primaeval concerns of life and survival, as an additional social norm, which will determine the future. Indeed it is about urgent changes with regard to our living conditions, but at first it is about the mobilisation of a broader elite of responsible thinkers, who think ahead as independently as possible and engage themselves bravely! Each one of us can belong to that elite. Only in this way the "public sphere", which was recognised by Habermas as the central source of stimulus for social transformation, can generate its necessary force. And again, as it happened so often in the history of mankind, we pin our hopes on our youth; the intelligent and consequent "agenda setting" towards sustainability should become one of their most noble tasks.

---

[12] We seem to believe, that we are able to secure our intelligence, education and creativity by living in a sort of tense coexistence with our computers. But there is no such coexistence. We need to let the computers do, what they can do, so that we ourselves become free to give them new orders.

[13] Perhaps the free will is an illusion and the computer models, which rebut it, are right. But it is an illusion, which ... benefits society, because it allows its continuing existence.

[14] It is about realities. In schools, universities and at workplaces the relation between master and servant, between humans and machines needs new determination.

8. The limited social conflict as important engine for social changes

In *"Pfade aus Utopia"* the more conservative European sociologist Ralf Dahrendorf has highlighted the necessity of social conflicts as great creative forces of social change (Dahrendorf 1974: 261). Yet, Dahrendorf puts is observation into perspective: *"Natürlich müssen wir nicht annehmen, dass Konflikte immer gewaltsam und unkontrolliert sind"*[15] (Dahrendorf 1974: 261). He also sees future social acting as a continuous social dialectic:

„…es mag sein, daß menschliche Gesellschaft in philosophischer Betrachtung stets zwei Gesichter von gleicher Wirklichkeit hat: eines der Stabilität, der Harmonie und des Consensus, und eines des Wandels, des Konfliktes und des Zwanges"[16] (Dahrendorf 1974: 262-263).

On the way to a society of sustainability we will, likewise, need this dualism of conflict and stability with the immanent ideal of new balances and will thus constantly encounter it. However, the perspective that this society, in a constructive and democratic sense might be able to deal with conflicts and can refrain from the excessive pressure of economic growth maximisation, without e.g. giving up the efficiency of already developed economic-technological instruments, seems equally desirable.

9. The approach of a "Third Way" with the goals of today

As already mentioned, a society of sustainability will not establish itself beyond the existing, economy and technology which has been developed throughout centuries.

The reformer Ota Šik, who had fought for a "Third Way" more than 40 years ago, had insistently warned with respect to changes of social systems against propagated *"Wunschvorstellungen einer Gesellschaftsform"*, *"in welcher der Mensch nicht mehr egoistische Ziele verfolgen sollte"*[17] (Sik 1973: 53).

Ota Šik back then:

"All solche Versuche werden heute ebenso wie vor hundert Jahren scheitern bzw. bloße Wunschträume bleiben, denn sie unterscheiden sich grundsätzlich nicht von den Utopien der Fouriers, Saint-Simons, Owens u.ä.. Der ökonomische Egoismus des Menschen ist ökonomisch bedingt und kann sich nur ge-

---

[15] Of course we don't need to assume, that conflicts are always violent and uncontrollable.

[16] *"…it may be, that human society from an philosophical point of view always displays two faces of equal reality: one of stability, of harmony and of consensus and one of change, of conflict and of coercion.*

[17] Wishful thinking of a social system in which the individual should no longer follow selfish goals.

mäß der ökonomischen Entwicklung langfristig in seinen Formen ändern"[18]
(Sik 1973: 53-54).

This economic moment of personal benefit can indeed also be a key to a
society of sustainability, especially if today's society, on the basis of
sound information, free, sovereign opinion-forming and democratically
carried out conflicts, provides the necessary framework conditions in
this respect and is thus able to indicate a constructive-sensible consumer
and producer culture. However, in his book *"Fortschrittsmythen"*[19], which
was written in the context of the energy crisis in 1973, Ivan Illich com-
ments rather critically on the possibility of an ecologically oriented and
economically based vision of society:

> *"Die spätindustrielle Gesellschaft organisiert das Leben um die Waren herum.
> Unsere marktintensiven Gesellschaften messen den materiellen Fortschritt an
> Hand der zunehmenden Menge und Vielfalt der produzierten Waren ... So-
> lange die ökologische Bewegung am Establishment orientiert ist, kann sie die-
> sen Trend nur verstärken; ..."*[20] (Illich 1978: 19).

With respect to the erosion processes for our worldwide future which
was already virulent at that time, Illich basically saw only two ways (Illich 1978: 27):

• Maintenance of the market-intense economic systems along with a
  change of the external design of its output;
• extensive reduction of our dependence on goods with new living
  conditions and modern tools, by which an increasing part of our
  needs can be directly satisfied.

Almost 40 years ago, when Illich postulated this, there might perhaps
theoretically still have been time for a worldwide fundamental change of
system in terms of an ethos of moderation (*"Ethos der Mäßigung"*, Illich
1978: 28), which was not as radical as the destruction approach of Carl
Amery.

Today, in light of the size of our environmental and social problems,
we need to seek a new Third Way, which in this century centrally has to

---

[18] All such attempts will fail today as they have done a hundred years ago or respectively will remain mere pipe dreams, because they do not differ from the utopias
by Fouriers, Saint-Simon, Owens or others. The economic egoism of humans is
economically conditioned and can only change its forms in the long run according
to the economic development.

[19] Titel original edition: „The Right to Useful Unemployment".

[20] The late industrial society organises life around goods. Our market-intense society
measures material progress due to the increasing amount and variety of produced
goods...as long as the ecological movement is oriented at the establishment, it can
only enhance this trend;...

be based on the ideas of adaptability, reformability and the use of our existing structures. But with a view to our plagued planet there is neither enough time left nor are there means for decades of oversized, inefficient and unclear social experiments.

The "Third Way" of the future is no longer the way in-between capitalism or socialism with their common homocentric, in their substance environmentally harmful mindsets, but the way between high economic, technologic and ecologic system efficiency and a society, which views its progress in the lasting and self-responsible preservation of a balance between humans and between humans and nature.

10. There is nothing good unless you do it

The discussions concerning strategic options for containing environmentally destructive economic developments have already been carried out during the nineteen seventies in the context of the first big oil crisis. Even at that time, one of the leading protagonists in that debate, Gunnar Myrdal, saw major problems, due to the systemic reduced reformability of traditional economic nations and their imitators. He also saw an important key to the necessary change in mobilizing the "public sphere" (see Habermas). Myrdal combined it especially with the desire to make this sphere systematically the central force of practical change:

"In Umweltfragen kommt es darauf an, die bedrohliche Gefahr jedermann vor Augen zu führen...Im nationalen Rahmen bedeutet das, wirklich willens zu sein, einen „neuen Lebensstil" anzunehmen"[21] (Myrdal, G. 1973: 13-44).

Additionally, he advocated international bodies with more competences.

After almost 40 years we assess that many trend-setters like the catalytic automobile, the expansion of alternative energies and the conclusion of climate agreements have come about, but in the end the depletion of nature worldwide and in our home countries has not been stopped, but accelerated. The "Global Footprint Network latest estimates conclude that humanity's demand in 2005 exceeded the regenerative capacity of the planet by about 30 per cent" (E.U. v. Weizsäcker 2009: 7). The projection of the "Global Footprint" until 2050 shows the current trend of our civilisation and the necessity of a real turning point.

---

[21] In environmental questions it is decisive to make everybody aware of the threatening danger ...Within national contexts this means being genuinely willing to adopt a "new lifestyle"... He additionally recommended to grant international bodies more competencies.

Figure 1: Ecological Footprint (1961-2050)

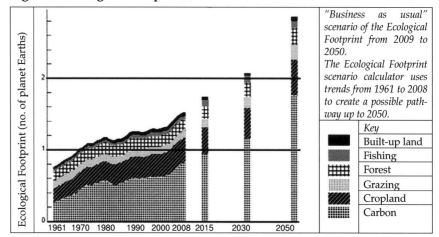

Source: Footprint Network Blog – Ecological Limits, http://www.footprintnetwork.org 06/05/2012 02:29 AM.

The clear call of the Intergovernmental Panel on Climate Change (IPCC) (cf. chapter 1) leaves no doubt: the human race has no time left to wait for lengthy learning and coordination processes. Therefore we need new methods to accelerate the processes of learning, acting and solving!

Nevertheless, in principle Myrdal was right with his postulate of a persistent self-socialisation as most stable condition for a successful change of the system.

With respect to this starting position a more consistent and more radical way is required – in terms of a fundament and an impetus for a greater move to a society of sustainability:

1. On the basis of international agreements (Rancun and subsequent conferences with fixed maximum values and generally binding instruments like the international emission trading) for this century the nations must define their sustainability-relevant national reduction targets as inviolable guidelines, e.g. from 2050 onward 80 % of all energy supply through alternative energies and until 2110 at the latest worldwide one tonne greenhouse gas per person per year.
2. These reduction targets must attain the rank of constitutional targets and thus need to become the object of an agreement binding for society as a whole in terms of its consistent fulfilment.
3. In order to achieve these goals, independent specialised bodies need to be established in support of the central government and the regional executives with an excellent periphery of experts, who are to be

integrated decisively into the development of a consistent master plan with the necessary decentralised elements and who are under the duty of annual public reporting to monitor implementation progress. Points of reference for this can be the 500 billion USD energy savings programme, which was developed for the Obama administration in 2009 (see E. U. v. Weizsäcker 2010: 108) or the 4 trillion RMB programme of the Chinese government for a national "smart grid" of 2009/2010 (Chinanews 30.12.2010).

4. The implementations of such programmes require the optimisation of the legal framework, the control systems, the state aid instruments and the efficient and systematic transformation of the entire system of economics in the sense of:
   - Decoupling of economic growth and resource consumption;
   - ecological innovation with job perspectives;
   - increasing efficiency respectively effectiveness of an ecological market economy;
   - strengthening of regional economic cycles ("closed loops");
   - optimal interaction in the international sphere (see Kleinert 1978: 143).

5. These fundamental rearrangements are only possible, if an inspiring "public sphere" takes full effect and at best does so through the behaviour of its propellant stakeholders:
   - Analogously to successful efforts like the value analysis, quality assurance and data protection, there should be working groups for sustainability and corresponding commissaries on all levels of the economic system and of state structures, which have to assume extensive impulse and controlling functions.
   - Within the framework of symposia, exhibitions, conferences and other suitable discussion forums, there must be comprehensive information and communication on all levels of society with respect to the targets of sustainability and the conditions for their achievement. In the course of this, also platforms of democratic parties and e.g. churches must be involved. The integration of the internet as information and opinion exchange (from "facebook" to "naturebook"!) is just as necessary as the critical-constructive participation of the independent press as the fourth estate and an important form of expression of the "public sphere" in modern society.
   - Across all generations we need to mobilise practice- and action-oriented motivators, initiators, implementors and supporters. This is an epochal challenge for parents, pre-schools, schools, universities and others responsible for education since sustainability-oriented behaviour can be made easily accessible, if individual acting has not

yet adopted rigid forms. The growing enthusiasm for Greenpeace, Robin Wood etc. indicates a great target person potential for such a perspective. Everywhere working and qualification programmes across generations should be developed for a sustainable society, in which voluntary and paid actors are installed to work for e.g. projects on species protection, the renaturation of river landscapes or the restoration of robust forests. Such positive experiences give the "public sphere" an enduring characteristic strength.

6. The entrepreneurship and especially the middle class businesses with their great number of small and medium-sized companies must play a very important role. This is not only a question of assuming a social or respectively an ecological responsibility, but more and more a question of entrepreneurial market profiling and of securing livelihood: "The world has turned green. Sustainability is more than just a business megatrend; ... We are experiencing a revolution, perhaps as profound as the industrial revolution, which altered every facet of life as it was known and understood ... Just like revolutions before it, the green revolution will destroy companies and wipe out industries that miss or ignore the signals." (Roland Berger Strategy Consultants 2011: 1)

The necessary development of regional economic cycles offers a particular chance to medium-sized enterprises, which have employees and a management available that are familiar with the regional problems and tasks due to their organisational focus. The Zeri method (see Panel-lecture by Markus Haastert and others from the Blue Economy movement), but also e.g. initiatives of local chambers of handicrafts and chambers of industry and commerce must help ensure that these enterprises become a sustainable motor of social change. This work can be decisively supplemented by socially relevant infrastructure companies, which must play an exemplary part, since they are especially able to reach and integrate a great number of citizens, due to their specific range of service[22].

7. In this increasingly threatening ecological situation, which to this global extent and with this relevance to existence portrays a new type of experience to very many people, traditional taboos in progress (e.g. the "holiness" of property and possession) and the deep internalised illusion of unlimited wealth can practically best be overcome by social awareness-raising alternative drafts.

At this point it is no longer about utopias of a perfect state as a whole, but about practical constellations of society, which at first may

---

[22] See Andreas Scholz-Fleischmann in this volume, pp. 141-146.

be of insular character, but then in particular assert themselves by becoming role models. Examples in this respect are:

- The gradual separation of the traditional employee companies in favour of proven new forms of autonomy and interpersonal cooperation (cf. Miegel 2011: 194-200).
- Overcoming the strict threefold division of one's career into study, work, retirement and the implementation of a regular retirement age at the age of at least 67 years.
- The revival of family and family and neighbour networks as agents of social tasks from child care to care of the elderly and nature care (ibid.: 205-209).
- The strengthening of widespread culture and its diversity as counterweight to mere consumption and selfish thinking of the traditional economic systems (ibid.: 215-219).

Such goals must be continuously forwarded and transformed into political practice.

A great dynamic of change arises especially, if economic ambitions can be connected in an easy comprehensible way to social security concerns in terms of ecology and respectively climate protection in the sense of a three-dimensional sustainability.

We should e.g. address the large section of the middle classes by offering them an attractive ppp-based old-age pension in return for additional private insurances in old age with pension contributions, which are exclusively invested in climate-friendly environmental projects like e.g. energy-efficient house refurbishments and wind farms with safe, tax-free reflows. This way billions of Euro investments in jobs can be effectively combined with climate protection and retirement provision, thus having a strong impact on society.

8. In the face of the excessive debts of nations along with their growing burden of climatically caused environmental damage and the scarcity of resources, their population problems ranging from overageing to overpopulation etc. we must set strict priorities with respect to the upcoming social change.

In Europe our investments in sustainability should put a clear emphasis on modern structures for clean energies, high energy efficiency and savings in order to develop a technological and economic competence for the future, which can help us ecologically and contributes to more jobs and more social security.

On this basis of clear and binding targets we must now evaluate the experiences of pilot projects and incorporate them into practice-oriented reference projects like e.g. in Friedrichshafen at Lake Constance (T-City Friedrichshafen) where smart meters are now being installed in every household in town for electricity, gas and water after 3 years of testing (see Telekom 2011).

Only due to this transparency with respect to daily energy consumption and need that has become possible now, smart grids and decentralised micro-grids, meaning intelligent networks, can provide the necessary energy in an optimal manner. Already by 2050 Germany should obtain at least 80 % of its energy from alternative energy resources with a volatility that requires a sensitive coordination of energy products, energy storage and cost-saving energy consumption.

With regard to the reference project communities it seems recommendable to assemble the different components for a sustainable city like alternative energy production, smart metering, smart grids, energy-efficient house refurbishment, e-mobility etc. individually step by step at each specific location in order to obtain an ideal interdependency.

Efforts in this direction are e.g. plans for Berlin (cf. *"Sustainable Urban Infrastructure"*-Study conducted by the TU Berlin with the support of Siemens AG and Vattenfall Europe AG in 2011) or – in the sense of a city from the retort – for Masdar City in Abu Dhabi, (see Siemens 2011; see Mogren 2009:100).

In each reference city a competence centre should collect the local experiences and provide – in cooperation with experts and specialist firms – a professional overview for those, who realize or plan to realize similar strategies at their site.

Similar to the 500 billion USD plan for the Obama administration in 2009, initiated by the Centre of American Progress and the Energy Future Coalition, a master plan for Europe in combination with individual national plans and based on preliminary work should include the following steps (see E. U. v. Weizsäcker 2010: 108; 39-44; see Gege 2011: 18, 63, 230-234):

- Development and networking of necessary management capacities;
- energetic stocktaking in the public and private sector including an analysis of population structure, of commuter flows, of consumer behaviour etc.;
- development of smart grid systems with alternative energy production solutions, smart metering and Green IT;
- realisation of energy-efficient house refurbishments by using proven contracting models in the public and private sector (most important fields of application: room heating and cooling, employment of energy-saving technologies, reduction of energy consumption in terms of hot water in line with innovative storage solutions, improvement of lighting);

- development of systems of sustainable mobility on the basis of electric cars as an integral element of a comprehensive public transportation offer (Canzler 2011: 45). But here too the ecological context must be taken into consideration, since the use phosphorus in automotive batteries can lead to a worldwide lack of biologically vital phosphorus and would be nutritionally dangerously disadvantageous (see H. Greuling, Sept. 5, 2011: 7);
- planning and building of "passive houses" and "zero energy houses" as part of public house building or state subsidies for the construction of private houses and commercial buildings;
- broad implementation of energy efficient lighting systems including street and sidewalk lighting and all types of billboards;
- reconstruction of industrial energy consumption systems (e.g. optimisation of pumps, electric motors, compressed air systems, ventilation technology, drying technology, cooling, water treatment, production processes, use of resources and preliminary products). With respect to the volatility of alternative energy sources like wind and sun especially the industry, which e.g. in Germany consumes over 50 percent of German energy in total, can make a major contribution to a successful change in our energy policy; Christof Bauer of Evonik Industries AG: "*In der Industrie gibt es ein hohes Potential, zur Stabilisierung der Netze beizutragen und zwar sowohl durch gezielten Mehr- als auch Minderverbrauch*"[23] (J. Schlandt, Sept. 1, 2011: 11).

11. We must not fail for lack of financing

The question of financing is one of the most popular "killer questions" in today's poltical discourse. It follows the line of argument that climate change has to wait just until we have the means to finance our rescue programmes. However nature doesn't act in accordance to our national finances.

Today's failures create an avalanche of problems with growing speed, which will in the long run overcharge our forces at some point. A quite possible increase of the average world temperature by 5°C and an increase of the sea level by 1 metre or more would cause severe incisions for billions of people for which neither our global and financial system nor its subsystems are prepared (see Potsdam-Institut für Klimafolgenforschung 2007: 11). That is why the means for the described measures must be made available *now*.

---

[23] There is a great potential in industry to contribute to stabilising the networks, both with respect to targeted increased consumption as well as to reduced consumption.

The inevitable rise of energy prices has the advantage that in all parts of society energy efficiency or, respectively, energy savings can lead to considerable lower costs. These savings of otherwise unavoidable costs also leave a leeway for the calculatory depreciations due to the manifold energy saving investments and their refunding.

It is the task of business studies to put forward the ideal business models along with an adequately attractive return on invest. In this respect a win-win-situation with regard to a sustainable society should be intended at all times. Respectively e.g. regarding investments in tenements both tenant and landlord should experience cost savings due to energy savings positively after amortisation. Energy saving must be fun for everyone, of course including the involved entrepreneurs.

The priority funding of this change in energy policy through the general tax system remains problematic, since national budgets follow the political logic that is oriented towards a comprehensive structure of executive duties rather than the top priority of climate protection. A typical example in this respect is the German "eco-tax", which is largely used to finance pension funds rather than for ecologic purposes. Furthermore, this way the request of the citizens to directly and transparently invest in climate protection or in other ecologic areas gets lost.

This leads to the recommendation to open up to other financing methods as central instruments of funding investments for an ecological future. They also better serve the principle of subsidiarity, which belongs to the basic principles of an ecological and social market economy and a citizen-centred society (see Grosser 1988). The author has introduced the instrument of the already mentioned „Klimaschutz-Rente"[24] in Germany as a reasonable solution for the subsidiary provision with a great funding volume (see J. Thomsen 2010).

The development in Germany shows that for many people, state pensions offer no sufficient financial security during retirement. Therefore, in Germany the Federal Government introduced the additional "Riester pension", which has already been able to acquire over 13 million pension savers (see Glossar/R/005__Riester-Rente 2011).

Unfortunately, only a very small fraction of environmental investments benefits from these subsidised capital investments. This could be changed by means of a specific "climate protection pension" and attractive investment conditions. In the future these private pension savings can simultaneously serve a green economy, personal retirement provisions and climate protection. In Europe this way three-digit billion Euro funds could be acquired.

---

[24] Climate protection pension.

The German environmental expert Maximilian Gege suggests to set up a "future fund" for Germany to which the majority of private households should contribute on a voluntary basis by deposits of 5-10% of their monetary assets in the following years. He recommends an interest rate of 5 percent. With a net-monetary asset of 3.300 billion Euro (2010) this would account for a sum of 165-330 billion Euro exclusively for climate protection investments in Germany (see Gege 2011: 224-244).

As with the "climate protection pension", the legal framework and the organisational implementation must be arranged in a way that sufficient incentives for such voluntary actions remain. In addition tax exempt amounts referring to payments in and/or payments out can be helpful.

However, it should be clear for everyone, that participation is voluntary, but nonetheless reality may request more restrictive solutions at some point.

12. Spiritual renewal as a task for science

The journalist Dirk C. Fleck has given a glimpse into the next decade with his novel *"Das Tahiti Projekt"* and has demonstrated, using the example of Tahiti, how a great deal of idealism can establish a sustainable society worth living in. In this novel the fictitious president of Tahiti, Omai, addresses UN representatives with words that turn out to be far more realistic than many of us would believe today:

"Die wichtigste Frage, die wir uns heute noch zu stellen haben, heißt: kollektiver Selbstmord oder geistige Erneuerung ... Unser Verständnis von Umweltschutz muss sich radikal ändern ... Bisher reden die meisten Regierungen von Beständen, wenn sie von der Natur sprechen. Sie machen in allem eine Rechnung auf ... Unsere Forderung, der natürlichen Mitwelt Respekt zu erweisen und ihren Eigenwert anzuerkennen, ist das Kernstück einer Ethik, die zur Leitlinie der gesamten Menschheit werden muss"[25] (Fleck 2007: 316-317).

It is about time that science as mainspring and treasury of mankind no longer leaves a comprehensive development and realisation of a society of sustainability up to literati alone. If not, our great-grandchildren will inhabit an earth that is much closer to the apocalypse than to paradise.

---

[25] The most important question we must ask ourselves today is: collective suicide or spiritual renewal ... Our understanding of environmental protection must change radically ... So far most governments talk about stocks, when they talk about nature. They tend to constantly do the sums ... Our demand to show some respect with regard to our fellow creatures and to recognize their intrinsic value is the core of an ethic, which should become the guideline for the whole of mankind.

References

Amery, C. 1976: Natur als Politik, Reinbek bei Hamburg

Blanning, T. C. W. 2002: The Culture of Power and the Power of Culture, Oxford

Blanning, T. C. W. 2006: Das Alte Europa 1660-1789. Kultur der Macht und Macht der Kultur, Darmstadt

Canzler, W., Knie, A. 2011: Einfach aufladen. Mit Elektromobilität in eine neue Zukunft, München

Chinanews 30.12.2010, http://www.chinanews.com/cj/2010/12-30/2758792.shtml accessed Sept. 14, 2011

Dahrendorf, R. 1974: Pfade aus Utopia, München

Erfahrungsbericht 2011 zum Erneuerbare-Energien-Gesetz (EEG Erfahrungsbericht) gemäß § 65 EEG, vorzulegen dem Deutschen Bundestag durch die Bundesregierung

Fleck, D. C. 2007: Das Tahiti Projekt, München

Gege, M., Heib, M. (ed.) 2011: Erfolgsfaktor Energieeffizienz – Investitionen, die sich lohnen, München

Gobal Footprint Network 2010: Ecological Footprint Atlas 2010, Oakland CA USA

Gray, J. 2010: Von Menschen und anderen Tieren, Stuttgart (Original edition 2002: Straw Dogs. Thoughts on Humans an other Animals, London)

Greuling, H. 2011: Phosphor ist eine Zeitbombe der Menschheit, in: Berliner Morgenpost, September 5, 2011, p. 7

Grosser, D., Lange, T., Müller-Armack, A., Neuss, B. 1988: Soziale Marktwirtschaft, Stuttgart

Glossar/R/005__Riester-Rente   2011: http://www.bundesfinanzministerium.de/nn_39846/DE/BMF__Startseite/Service/Glossar/R/005__Riester-Rente.html (accessed Sept. 13, 2011)

Footprint Network Blog 2012: http://www.footprintnetwork.org/en/index.php/ GFN/blog/gcat/ecological_limits/ (accessed May 31, 2012)

Telekom 2011: http://www.telekom.com/dtag/cms/content/dt/de/217308 (accessed Sept. 13, 2011)

Illich, I. 1978: Fortschrittsmythen, Reinbek bei Hamburg, (original edition 1974: The Right to Useful Unemployment, London)

Intergovernmental Panel on Climate Change IPCC, WMO/UNEP 2008: Climate Change 2007: Synthesis Report; translated and published by the Deutsche IPCC-Koordinierungsstelle Klimaänderung 2007 Syntheseberichte, Stuttgart

Kleinert, H., Mosdorf, S. 1998: Die Renaissance der Politik, Berlin

Miegel, M. 2011: EXIT Wohlstand ohne Wachstum, Berlin

Mogren, A., Fahnestock,A. 2009: A ONE TONNE FUTURE, Värnamo

Myrdal, G. 1973: Ökonomie einer verbesserten Umwelt, in: Nussbaum, H.v. (ed.), Die Zukunft des Wachstums, Düsseldorf, pp. 13-44

Nussbaum, H. v. (ed.) 1973: Die Zukunft des Wachstums, Düsseldorf

Postman, N. 1985: Wir amüsieren uns zu Tode, Frankfurt am Main (original edition 1985: Amusing Ourselves to Death, New York)

Potsdam-Institut für Klimafolgenforschung 2007: Himmel und Erde. Von Pergamon nach Potsdam, Potsdam

Richter, H. E. 2010: Moral in Zeiten der Krise, Berlin

Roland Berger Strategy Consultants 2011: Green Growth, Green Profit, London

Schirrmacher, F. 2009: Payback, München
Schlandt, J. 2011: Die Industrie als Puffer, in: Berliner Zeitung, Sept. 1, 2011, p. 11
Siemens AG, Vattenfall Europe AG (ed.) 2011: Sustainable Urban Infrastructure, study, Berlin
Šik, O. 1973: Argumente für den Dritten Weg, Hamburg
Stiglitz, J., 2002: Globalization and its discontents, London
Thomsen, J. 2010: Henkel winkt mit dem grünen Zaunpfahl, in: Berliner Zeitung, March 24, 2010, http://www.berlinonline.de/berliner-zeitung/archiv/.bin/dump.fcgi/2010/0324/berlin/0024/index.html (accessed March 24, 2010)
Weizsäcker, C. F. v. 1978: Deutlichkeit, München
Weizsäcker, E. U. v., Hargroves, K., Smith, M. 2009: Factor Five. Transforming the Global Economy through 80 % Improvements in Ressource Productivity, London
Weizsäcker, E. U. v., Hargroves, K., Smith, M. 2010: Faktor Fünf. Die Formel für nachhaltiges Wachstum, München

INFRASTRUCTURE ECONOMY AS A NUCLEUS FOR MORE SUSTAINABILITY

ANDREAS SCHOLZ-FLEISCHMANN
(BERLIN, GERMANY)

The infrastructure economy of the 19th century has laid the basis of to-day´s power supply nets, traffic tracks and pipelines. These decisions are very long term - even if they were not originally made with sustainabil-ity in mind. Infrastructure companies today must be aware of the im-portance of their actions for sustainability. More than that - they should be a driver of innovation and sustainability since they remain the basis for many other corporate and investment decisions.

Infrastructure companies in the public sector have a special responsi-bility, because they do not have to serve the interests of private share-holders. Instead, these public companies are responsible to their public owners – the citizens, represented by politicians – and have to serve the overall interests of a community. The environmental and social impacts of large investment decisions are prominent issues today. When projects do not communicate properly about these topics, or even fail to take them into consideration, they can run into difficulties.

A consequence of many new technologies is that consumers, as well as producers, wait for the development of a related infrastructure. Con-sumers will, for example, hinge their willingness to purchase electric or hybrid vehicles on "affordable" car prices and a network of charging sta-tions. Affordable prices in turn depend on the fact that cars can be pro-duced in large scale. The motor vehicle industry will base their own de-cisions on the existence of charging stations and consumers' willingness to buy. If the infrastructure companies – in this example the energy sup-pliers – refrain from investing in charging stations until an appropriate number of vehicles is on the roads, then the vicious circle is complete.

If a political consensus for the use of a new technology exists, then the infrastructure companies have to be the driver. Companies increasingly have the task within their corporate social responsibility (CSR) to take responsibility for society or their region.

The classic "textbook" division of labor between politics and econo-mics does not work (anymore?) – i.e. the perfect structure of a democrat-ically elected government, which determines basic conditions for the economy, balances policy goals and social policy measures against an economic sector in which the "invisible hand", based on self-interest and competition, is given free reign. This is the best way for a community to function, but this structure seems to be disturbed.

Figure 1: Ideal Roles of Government and Economy

The impairments affect both sides; the national government no longer makes decisions independently, and even when it does such decisions are subject to significant risks. Populism is a key point here. The increasing complexity of issues (e.g. energy policy) is also an obstacle.

In regards to the economy, it has become clear that the hope that external costs are internalized through prices is not justified. Some processes (e.g. climate change) appear almost irreversible after they are realized. A "pricing" of the use of the environment according to the ideas of environmental economics does not work in those cases. Thus the relationship between economics and politics needs to be redefined if it is to lead to an overall social optimum.

Figure 2: Current Situation

In the following, I will concentrate on the responsibility of companies. The EU Commission has set the basis for this with its concept of CSR.

In 2011, the Commission expressed a new definition of CSR as "the responsibility of enterprises for their impacts on society" (European Commission 2011, p. 6). "To fully meet their corporate social responsibility, enterprises should have in place a process to integrate social, environmental, ethical, human rights and consumer concerns into their business operations and core strategy in close collaboration with their stakeholders, with the aim of:

- maximising the creation of shared value for their owners/ shareholders and for their other stakeholders and society at large;
- identifying, preventing and mitigating their possible adverse impacts" (European Commission 2011, p. 6).

For the Berlin Waste Management and Street-Cleaning Company (BSR) social and environmental responsibility is a high ranking strategic goal, and has been for years. We translate that into the following topics:

- In the social area:
  - o Investments in health and employability of our employees;
  - o encouragement of the employee´s work life balance;
  - o dealing with the impacts of demographic change;
  - o investments in education, training and re-training;
  - o consideration of our clients´ interests – which e.g. are getting older, too.
- In the environmental area:
  - o Promotion of the energy turnaround;
  - o investment in new technologies;
  - o reduced consumption of fossil energy;
  - o modernizing insulation of buildings;
  - o reduction of our carbon footprint.

We believe that companies' annual balance sheets should be complemented by reports on their environmental impacts and carbon footprints. Some companies are pioneers in this area today and we also add some information about these impacts in our annual report. In addition, we publish a report every two years on the company´s efforts to foster sustainability. We believe that this also makes sense economically speaking, since some companies have damaged their public image and lost clients and job candidates due to their reluctance toward embracing topics like environmental protection, fair trade, open information policy, etc.

BSR exemplifies the efforts an infrastructure company can, and should, undertake to promote sustainability in the following way:

First, we analyzed the areas in which we have the greatest impact on the environment. In addition, we assessed the social topics relevant to our employees and Berlin as a whole. In light of our analyses, the following areas are a focus of our attention.

Figure 3: BSR Vehicles

Car pool of BSR – ecological orientation   Ecology

- Vehicles are low-emission
- We use 100 garbage trucks with CNG today, from next year on we will use our own bio gas for the whole fleet of 150 trucks that we produce from bio waste
- We just now test the world's first garbage truck with fuel cell (hydrogen)
- Together with Daimler we test a hybrid garbage truck (electro/Diesel)
- We changed over to e-mobility with the first passenger cars

Environment/Climate
- Logistics: Our fleet consisted mainly of diesel-powered trucks, overall we have spent around 8 million liters of diesel oil per year. How can we reduce emissions in the long term and avoid fossil fuels?
- Energy consumption and production: On the one hand, we use energy, on the other hand, we are self-producers, such as in our waste-to-energy plant. How can we improve both?
- Building renovation: The properties of BSR are predominantly old buildings that were not perfectly restored and have very little insulation.
- Biowaste: We collect 60,000 tons of organic waste per year, which is now composted. The biogas contained therein is not used yet. In the process it escapes into the environment and is harmful to the climate.

Social issues
- Demography: The average age of our workforce is relatively high (47 years) considering that we have a large share of hard work in the city's streets. As the retirement age was raised to 67: How will we manage that?

- Health: How do we avoid health problems by heavy physical work that could end in a high loss of employability and rising costs?
- Training: In Berlin, there is still a significant percentage of youth unemployment. Especially young people with no education have little chance.

Figure 4: Final Stage of Organic Waste Disposal

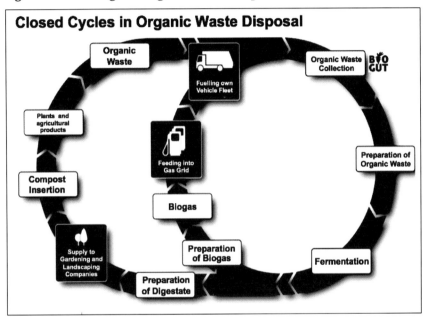

Our company has projects in progress or already completed for all of these issues. We, for instance, together with manufacturers, test drive new vehicle technologies like electric, hybrid and fuel cell vehicles.

From 2013 onward, we will treat the collected organic waste of our city in a new plant. We will produce biogas that 150 garbage trucks will run on. This will be a very concrete example of closed loops in our industry. In the coming years, we will improve our carbon footprint even more – we were able to reduce it by 70% since the year 2000. Furthermore, 3,700m^2 solar collectors are already installed today; they alone made possible savings in some 1,500 tons of CO_2 per year.

The management of demographic change is also complex. In addition to numerous prevention programs for employees and a health care system, the BSR has a retirement program put in place for the highly stressed employees who move heavy bins or are used in street cleaning.

Those employees, having reached the age of 55, can go to 50% part-time work, with the result that they are working five years full time and can stay home the second 5 years. The company pays 80 percent of their income over the whole period.

All of these measures are not just a function of CSR. They also address issues that are of considerable importance for the company and have significantly increased the reputation of the "brand" BSR in Berlin's population.

Reference

European Commission 2011: COM(2011) 681 final (*Communication from the Commission to the European Parliament, the Council, the European Economic and Social Committee and the Committee of the Regions*): A renewed EU strategy 2011-14 for Corporate Social Responsibility, Brussels, October 25, 2011

ATTACHMENT:

EDITORS and CONTRIBUTORS

Baccarella, Christian, Dipl.-Kfm., Friedrich-Alexander-University Erlangen- Nuremberg, chair for industrial management, Nuremberg (Germany), *baccarella@industrial-management*

Bartocci, Luca, Assoc. Prof., University of Perugia, Faculty of Economics, Perugia (Italy), *lbarto@unipg.it*

Chobanov, George, Prof. Dr., Sofia University "St. Kliment Ohridski", Faculty of Economics and Business Administration, Sofia (Bulgaria), *georgech@feb.uni-sofia.bg*

Flämig, Dieter, Prof. Dr., Dipl.-Ing., chairman of Infrawind Eurasia e.V., Berlin (Germany), *info@infrawind.com*

Gaulden, Corbett F., Prof. Dr., Angelo State University, College of Business, Dean and Professor of Marketing, San Angelo, Texas (USA), *corbett.gaulden@angelo.edu*

Gern, Jean-Pierre, Prof. (em.) Dr., University of Neuchâtel (Switzerland), *jean-pierre.gern@unine.ch*

Hohenadl, Stephan, Dipl.-Kfm., Senior Consultant at Simon-Kucher & Partners, Bonn (Germany), *bonn@simon-kucher.com*

Iankova, Stefka, Ph.D. student at Sofia University St. Kliment Ohridski, Faculty of Economics and Business Administration, Sofia (Bulgaria), *stefkaiankova2002@yahoo.com*

Picciaia, Francesca, Dr., University of Perugia, Faculty of Economics, Perugia (Italy), *picciaia@unipg.it*

Plöhn, Jürgen, Prof. Dr., EBC University of Applied Sciences Hamburg and Martin-Luther-University Halle-Wittenberg, Institute for Political Science and Japanese Studies, Halle (Germany), *ploehn.juergen@ebc-hochschule.de*

Scheiner, Christian, Dr., Friedrich-Alexander-University Erlangen-Nuremberg, chair for industrial management, Nuremberg (Germany), *scheiner@industrial-management.org*

Scholz-Fleischmann, Andreas, member of the executive board of the Berliner Stadtreinigung (BSR), Berlin (Germany), *service@BSR.de*

Schwalbach, Joachim, Prof. Dr., Humboldt-University Berlin, Faculty of Economics, Institute for Management, Berlin (Germany), *schwal@wiwi.hu-berlin.de*

Sedlarski, Teodor, Assoc. Prof. Dr., Sofia University "St. Kliment Ohridski", Faculty of Economics and Business Administration, Vice Dean for Academic Affairs and International Relations, Sofia (Bulgaria), *sedlarski@feb.uni-sofia.bg*

Voigt, Kai-Ingo, Prof. Dr., Friedrich-Alexander-Universität Erlangen-Nürnberg, Faculty of Law and Economics, chair for industrial management, Nuremberg (Germany), *voigt@industrial-management.org*

Sofia Conferences on Social and Economic Development in Europe

Editors: Prof. Dr. George Chobanov, Prof. Dr. Jürgen Plöhn,
Prof. Dr. Horst Schellhaass

Band 1   George Chobanov / Jürgen Plöhn / Horst Schellhaass (eds.): Towards a Knowledge-Based
Society in Europe. 10th International Conference on Policies of Economic and Social
Development, Sofia, October 5 to 7, 2007. 2009.

Band 2   George Chobanov / Jürgen Plöhn / Horst Schellhaass (eds.): Policies of Economic and
Social Development in Europe. 11th Annual Conference of the Faculty of Economics and
Business Administration. Dedicated to the 120th Anniversary of St. Kliment Ohridski
University of Sofia, Sofia, October 10 to 11, 2008. 2010.

Band 3   George Chobanov / Jürgen Plöhn / Horst Schellhaass (eds.): Markets, Sustainability and
Social Welfare Enhancement in the European Union. 12th and 13th Annual Conference of
the Faculty of Economics and Business Administration. Sofia, October 9 to 10, 2009 and
October 8 to 9, 2010. 2012.

Band 4   George Chobanov / Jürgen Plöhn (eds.): Crisis and Sustainability: Responses from Different
Positions. 14th Annual Conference of the Faculty of Economics and Business Administration.
Sofia, 7-8 October 2011. 2013.

www.peterlang.com